Abnormality Assessment Form

Date: _____   Evaluation Area: _____

T0111893

Abnormality	Number	Evaluation Criteria	Rank these items from 1 through 5: 5 being well done	Score (1-5)	Ideas / Suggestions / Comments
MINOR FLAWS	I	• Damage	Cracking, crushing, deformation, chipping, bending, etc.		
	II	• Play, Slackness	Movement, falling out, tilting, eccentricity, distortion, corrosion; Drive belts, Drive chains, cables, etc.		
	III	• Abnormal phenomena	Unusual noise, overheating, vibration, strange smells, discoloration, incorrect pressure, etc.		
	IV	• Adhesion	Accumulation of debris, peeling, malfunction, etc.		
	V	• Contamination; Damage	Light powder, accumulation of dirt, rust, grease, oil; impact areas, dents, scratches, scuffs, etc.		
			Minor Flaws: Category Subtotal:	Score: divided by 5	
UNFULFILLED BASIC CONDITIONS	VI	• Lubrication	Insufficient lubrication, dirty oil, undetermined liquid, or leaking lubricant, etc.		
	VII	• Lubricant supply	Lubricant inlets; dirty, damaged, or deformed, faulty pipes, etc.		
	VIII	• Oil level guages	Dirty, leaking, or damaged, no measurement of correct level, etc.		
	IX	• Tightening	Fasteners; nuts, bolts; loose, missing, cross-threaded, crushed, corroded, etc.		
			Unfulfilled Basic Conditions: Category Subtotal:	Score: divided by 4	
INACCESSIBLE PLACES	X	• Cleaning	Machine, covers, space, layout of machine, space to be able to clean, etc.		
	XI	• Checking	Able to check, layout, instrument location, position and orientation, operating-range known, etc.		
	XII	• Lubricating	Location and position of lubricant nipples, height, lubricant outlet, enough space, etc.		
	XIII	• Operation	Machine layout; position of valves, switches and levers, etc.		
	XIV	• Adjustment	For adjustment, position of gauges, thermometers, flow-meters, moisture and vacuum gauges, etc.		
			Inaccessible Places: Category Subtotal:	Score: divided by 5	
CONTAMINATION SOURCES	XV	• Product, Raw material	Leaks from products, spilling and mixing product type; Scattered material, too much material, etc.		
	XVI	• Lubricants	Mixing with product, leaks causing contamination, seeping oils, fluids, etc.		
	XVII	• Gases	Lack of pressure, leaking air, gases, steam, vapors, exhaust fumes, etc.		
	XVIII	• Liquids	Leaking waste liquids, not cleaning with solvents, contaminates not out of fluids, etc.		
	XIX	• Scrap, Other	Dunnage, cuttings, non-conforming parts, contaminants by people, forklifts, etc.		
			Contamination Sources: Category Subtotal:	Score: divided by 5	
QUALITY DEFECT SOURCES	XX	• Moisture	Moisture source, too much, too little, infiltration, temperature change, humidity change, etc.		
	XXI	• Grain size	Right sized filters, old filters, defective filters, operation not considered, etc.		
	XXII	• Concentration, Viscosity	Inadequate acclimation, pre-heating, compounding; Mixing, evaporation, accumulation, stirring, etc.		
	XXIII	• Foreign matter, Shock	Inclusion, entrant of contaminants, chips, scraps; Dropping, jolting, collision, vibration, etc.		
			Quality Defect Sources: Category Subtotal:	Score: divided by 4	
UNNECESSARY AND NON-URGENT ITEMS	XXIV	• Machinery	Evaluate the hydraulic pumps, their fans, compressors, support columns, tanks, etc.		
	XXV	• Piping equipment	Address pipes, hoses, ducts, valves, dampers, etc.		
	XXVI	• Measuring instruments	Temperatures, pressure gauges, vacuum gauges, amp-meters, etc.		
	XXVII	• Electrical equipment	Wiring, piping, power leads, switches, plugs, etc.		
	XXVIII	• Jigs and tools	General tools, cutting tools, jigs, molds, dies, frames, etc.		
			Unnecessary and Non-urgent Items: Category Subtotal:	Score: divided by 5	
UNSAFE PLACES	XXIX	• Floors	Cracks, uneven floors, objects, peeling of material, etc.		
	XXX	• Steps	No slip, no handrails, Irregular, uneven, too thin, slippery, etc.		
	XXXI	• Lights	Lack of lighting, no protection, dusty and grimy covers, missing lights, etc.		
	XXXII	• Rotating machinery	No protective covers, safety lines, safety cages, no emergency stops, etc.		
	XXXIII	• Lifting gear, Other	Location of hazards, wires, nail heads, split corners, other parts; Solvents, toxic gases, danger signs.		
			Unsafe Places: Category Subtotal:	Score: divided by 5	
				Total "Category Subtotals" Divided by 33 Score: TOTAL	

Abnormality Assessment Form

Date: _____ Evaluation Area: _____

Abnormality	Number	Evaluation Criteria	Rank these items from 1 through 5: 5 being well done	Score (1-5)	Ideas / Suggestions / Comments
MINOR FLAWS	I	• Damage	Cracking, crushing, deformation, chipping, bending, etc.		
	II	• Play, Slackness	Movement, falling out, tilting, eccentricity, distortion, corrosion; Drive belts, Drive chains, cables, etc.		
	III	• Abnormal phenomena	Unusual noise, overheating, vibration, strange smells, discoloration, incorrect pressure, etc.		
	IV	• Adhesion	Accumulation of debris, peeling, malfunction, etc.		
	V	• Contamination; Damage	Light powder, accumulation of dirt, rust, grease, oil; impact areas, dents, scratches, scuffs, etc.		
			Minor Flaws: Category Subtotal:	Score: divided by 5	
UNFULFILLED BASIC CONDITIONS	VI	• Lubrication	Insufficient lubrication, dirty oil, undetermined liquid, or leaking lubricant, etc.		
	VII	• Lubricant supply	Lubricant inlets; dirty, damaged, or deformed, faulty pipes, etc.		
	VIII	• Oil level guages	Dirty, leaking, or damaged, no measurement of correct level, etc.		
	IX	• Tightening	Fasteners; nuts, bolts; loose, missing, cross-threaded, crushed, corroded, etc.		
			Unfulfilled Basic Conditions: Category Subtotal:	Score: divided by 4	
INACCESSIBLE PLACES	X	• Cleaning	Machine, covers, space, layout of machine, space to be able to clean, etc.		
	XI	• Checking	Able to check, layout, instrument location, position and orientation, operating-range known, etc.		
	XII	• Lubricating	Location and position of lubricant nipples, height, lubricant outlet, enough space, etc.		
	XIII	• Operation	Machine layout; position of valves, switches and levers, etc.		
	XIV	• Adjustment	For adjustment, position of gauges, thermometers, flow-meters, moisture and vacuum gauges, etc.		
			Inaccessible Places: Category Subtotal:	Score: divided by 5	
CONTAMINATION SOURCES	XV	• Product, Raw material	Leaks from products, spilling and mixing product type; Scattered material, too much material, etc.		
	XVI	• Lubricants	Mixing with product, leaks causing contamination, seeping oils, fluids, etc.		
	XVII	• Gases	Lack of pressure, leaking air, gases, steam, vapors, exhaust fumes, etc.		
	XVIII	• Liquids	Leaking waste liquids, not cleaning with solvents, contaminates not out of fluids, etc.		
	XIX	• Scrap, Other	Dunnage, cuttings, non-conforming parts, contaminants by people, forklifts, etc.		
			Contamination Sources: Category Subtotal:	Score: divided by 5	
QUALITY DEFECT SOURCES	XX	• Moisture	Moisture source, too much, too little, infiltration, temperature change, humidity change, etc.		
	XXI	• Grain size	Right sized filters, old filters, defective filters, operation not considered, etc.		
	XXII	• Concentration, Viscosity	Inadequate acclimation, pre-heating, compounding; Mixing, evaporation, accumulation, stirring, etc.		
	XXIII	• Foreign matter, Shock	Inclusion, entrant of contaminants, chips, scraps; Dropping, jolting, collision, vibration, etc.		
			Quality Defect Sources: Category Subtotal:	Score: divided by 4	
UNNECESSARY AND NON-URGENT ITEMS	XXIV	• Machinery	Evaluate the hydraulic pumps, their fans, compressors, support columns, tanks, etc.		
	XXV	• Piping equipment	Address pipes, hoses, ducts, valves, dampers, etc.		
	XXVI	• Measuring instruments	Temperatures, pressure gauges, vacuum gauges, amp-meters, etc.		
	XXVII	• Electrical equipment	Wiring, piping, power leads, switches, plugs, etc.		
	XXVIII	• Jigs and tools	General tools, cutting tools, jigs, molds, dies, frames, etc.		
			Unnecessary and Non-urgent Items: Category Subtotal:	Score: divided by 5	
UNSAFE PLACES	XXIX	• Floors	Cracks, uneven floors, objects, peeling of material, etc.		
	XXX	• Steps	No slip, no handrails, irregular, uneven, too thin, slippery, etc.		
	XXXI	• Lights	Lack of lighting, no protection, dusty and grimy covers, missing lights, etc.		
	XXXII	• Rotating machinery	No protective covers, safety lines, safety cages, no emergency stops, etc.		
	XXXIII	• Lifting gear, Other	Location of hazards, wires, nail heads, split corners, other parts; Solvents, toxic gases, danger signs.		
			Unsafe Places: Category Subtotal:	Score: divided by 5	

Total "Category Subtotals" Divided by 33 Score: TOTAL

Abnormality Assessment Form

Date: _____   Evaluation Area: _____

Abnormality	Number	Evaluation Criteria	Rank these items from 1 through 5: 5 being well done	Score (1-5)	Ideas / Suggestions / Comments
MINOR FLAWS	I	• Damage	Cracking, crushing, deformation, chipping, bending, etc.		
	II	• Play, Slackness	Movement, falling out, tilting, eccentricity, distortion, corrosion; Drive belts, Drive chains, cables, etc.		
	III	• Abnormal phenomena	Unusual noise, overheating, vibration, strange smells, discoloration, incorrect pressure, etc.		
	IV	• Adhesion	Accumulation of debris, peeling, malfunction, etc.		
	V	• Contamination; Damage	Light powder, accumulation of dirt, rust, grease, oil; impact areas, dents, scratches, scuffs, etc.		
			Minor Flaws: Category Subtotal: **Score: divided by 5**		
UNFULFILLED BASIC CONDITIONS	VI	• Lubrication	Insufficient lubrication, dirty oil, undetermined liquid, or leaking lubricant, etc.		
	VII	• Lubricant supply	Lubricant inlets; dirty, damaged, or deformed, faulty pipes, etc.		
	VIII	• Oil level guages	Dirty, leaking, or damaged, no measurement of correct level, etc.		
	IX	• Tightening	Fasteners; nuts, bolts; loose, missing, cross-threaded, crushed, corroded, etc.		
			Unfulfilled Basic Conditions: Category Subtotal: **Score: divided by 4**		
INACCESSIBLE PLACES	X	• Cleaning	Machine, covers, space, layout of machine, space to be able to clean, etc.		
	XI	• Checking	Able to check, layout, instrument location, position and orientation, operating-range known, etc.		
	XII	• Lubricating	Location and position of lubricant nipples, height, lubricant outlet, enough space, etc.		
	XIII	• Operation	Machine layout; position of valves, switches and levers, etc.		
	XIV	• Adjustment	For adjustment, position of gauges, thermometers, flow-meters, moisture and vacuum gauges, etc.		
			Inaccessible Places: Category Subtotal: **Score: divided by 5**		
CONTAMINATION SOURCES	XV	• Product, Raw material	Leaks from products, spilling and mixing product type; Scattered material, too much material, etc.		
	XVI	• Lubricants	Mixing with product, leaks causing contamination, seeping oils, fluids, etc.		
	XVII	• Gases	Lack of pressure, leaking air, gases, steam, vapors, exhaust fumes, etc.		
	XVIII	• Liquids	Leaking waste liquids, not cleaning with solvents, contaminates not out of fluids, etc.		
	XIX	• Scrap, Other	Dunnage, cuttings, non-conforming parts, contaminants by people, forklifts, etc.		
			Contamination Sources: Category Subtotal: **Score: divided by 5**		
QUALITY DEFECT SOURCES	XX	• Moisture	Moisture source, too much, too little, infiltration, temperature change, humidity change, etc.		
	XXI	• Grain size	Right sized filters, old filters, defective filters, operation not considered, etc.		
	XXII	• Concentration, Viscosity	Inadequate acclimation, pre-heating, compounding; Mixing, evaporation, accumulation, stirring, etc.		
	XXIII	• Foreign matter, Shock	Inclusion, entrant of contaminants, chips, scraps; Dropping, jolting, collision, vibration, etc.		
			Quality Defect Sources: Category Subtotal: **Score: divided by 4**		
UNNECESSARY AND NON-URGENT ITEMS	XXIV	• Machinery	Evaluate the hydraulic pumps, their fans, compressors, support columns, tanks, etc.		
	XXV	• Piping equipment	Address pipes, hoses, ducts, valves, dampers, etc.		
	XXVI	• Measuring instruments	Temperatures, pressure gauges, vacuum gauges, amp-meters, etc.		
	XXVII	• Electrical equipment	Wiring, piping, power leads, switches, plugs, etc.		
	XXVIII	• Jigs and tools	General tools, cutting tools, jigs, molds, dies, frames, etc.		
			Unnecessary and Non-urgent Items: Category Subtotal: **Score: divided by 5**		
UNSAFE PLACES	XXIX	• Floors	Cracks, uneven floors, objects, peeling of material, etc.		
	XXX	• Steps	No slip, no handrails, irregular, uneven, too thin, slippery, etc.		
	XXXI	• Lights	Lack of lighting, no protection, dusty and grimy covers, missing lights, etc.		
	XXXII	• Rotating machinery	No protective covers, safety lines, safety cages, no emergency stops, etc.		
	XXXIII	• Lifting gear, Other	Location of hazards, wires, nail heads, split corners, other parts; Solvents, toxic gases, danger signs.		
			Unsafe Places: Category Subtotal: **Score: divided by 5**		**Total "Category Subtotals" Divided by 33 Score: TOTAL**

Abnormality Assessment Form

Date: _____ Evaluation Area: _____

Abnormality	Number	Evaluation Criteria	Rank these items from 1 through 5: 5 being well done	Score (1-5)	Ideas / Suggestions / Comments
MINOR FLAWS	I	• Damage	Cracking, crushing, deformation, chipping, bending, etc.		
	II	• Play, Slackness	Movement, falling out, tilting, eccentricity, distortion, corrosion; Drive belts, Drive chains, cables, etc.		
	III	• Abnormal phenomena	Unusual noise, overheating, vibration, strange smells, discoloration, incorrect pressure, etc.		
	IV	• Adhesion	Accumulation of debris, peeling, malfunction, etc.		
	V	• Contamination; Damage	Light powder, accumulation of dirt, rust, grease, oil; impact areas, dents, scratches, scuffs, etc.		
		Minor Flaws: Category Subtotal:		Score: divided by 5	
UNFULFILLED BASIC CONDITIONS	VI	• Lubrication	Insufficient lubrication, dirty oil, undetermined liquid, or leaking lubricant, etc.		
	VII	• Lubricant supply	Lubricant inlets; dirty, damaged, or deformed, faulty pipes, etc.		
	VIII	• Oil level guages	Dirty, leaking, or damaged, no measurement of correct level, etc.		
	IX	• Tightening	Fasteners; nuts, bolts; loose, missing, cross-threaded, crushed, corroded, etc.		
		Unfulfilled Basic Conditions: Category Subtotal:		Score: divided by 4	
INACCESSIBLE PLACES	X	• Cleaning	Machine, covers, space, layout of machine, space to be able to clean, etc.		
	XI	• Checking	Able to check, layout, instrument location, position and orientation, operating-range known, etc.		
	XII	• Lubricating	Location and position of lubricant nipples, height, lubricant outlet, enough space, etc.		
	XIII	• Operation	Machine layout; position of valves, switches and levers, etc.		
	XIV	• Adjustment	For adjustment, position of gauges, thermometers, flow-meters, moisture and vacuum gauges, etc.		
		Inaccessible Places: Category Subtotal:		Score: divided by 5	
CONTAMINATION SOURCES	XV	• Product, Raw material	Leaks from products, spilling and mixing product type; Scattered material, too much material, etc.		
	XVI	• Lubricants	Mixing with product, leaks causing contamination, seeping oils, fluids, etc.		
	XVII	• Gases	Lack of pressure, leaking air, gases, steam, vapors, exhaust fumes, etc.		
	XVIII	• Liquids	Leaking waste liquids, not cleaning with solvents, contaminates not out of fluids, etc.		
	XIX	• Scrap, Other	Dunnage, cuttings, non-conforming parts, contaminants by people, forklifts, etc.		
		Contamination Sources: Category Subtotal:		Score: divided by 5	
QUALITY DEFECT SOURCES	XX	• Moisture	Moisture source, too much, too little, infiltration, temperature change, humidity change, etc.		
	XXI	• Grain size	Right sized filters, old filters, defective filters, operation not considered, etc.		
	XXII	• Concentration, Viscosity	Inadequate acclimation, pre-heating, compounding; Mixing, evaporation, accumulation, stirring, etc.		
	XXIII	• Foreign matter, Shock	Inclusion, entrant of contaminants, chips, scraps; Dropping, jolting, collision, vibration, etc.		
		Quality Defect Sources: Category Subtotal:		Score: divided by 4	
UNNECESSARY AND NON-URGENT ITEMS	XXIV	• Machinery	Evaluate the hydraulic pumps, their fans, compressors, support columns, tanks, etc.		
	XXV	• Piping equipment	Address pipes, hoses, ducts, valves, dampers, etc.		
	XXVI	• Measuring instruments	Temperatures, pressure gauges, vacuum gauges, amp-meters, etc.		
	XXVII	• Electrical equipment	Wiring, piping, power leads, switches, plugs, etc.		
	XXVIII	• Jigs and tools	General tools, cutting tools, jigs, molds, dies, frames, etc.		
		Unnecessary and Non-urgent Items: Category Subtotal:		Score: divided by 5	
UNSAFE PLACES	XXIX	• Floors	Cracks, uneven floors, objects, peeling of material, etc.		
	XXX	• Steps	No slip, no handrails, irregular, uneven, too thin, slippery, etc.		
	XXXI	• Lights	Lack of lighting, no protection, dusty and grimy covers, missing lights, etc.		
	XXXII	• Rotating machinery	No protective covers, safety lines, safety cages, no emergency stops, etc.		
	XXXIII	• Lifting gear, Other	Location of hazards, wires, nail heads, split corners, other parts; Solvents, toxic gases, danger signs.		
		Unsafe Places: Category Subtotal:		Score: divided by 5	

Total "Category Subtotals" Divided by 33 Score: TOTAL

Abnormality Assessment Form

Date: _____   Evaluation Area: _____

Abnormality	Number	Evaluation Criteria	Rank these items from 1 through 5: 5 being well done	Score (1-5)	Ideas / Suggestions / Comments
MINOR FLAWS	I	• Damage	Cracking, crushing, deformation, chipping, bending, etc.		
	II	• Play, Slackness	Movement, falling out, tilting, eccentricity, distortion, corrosion; Drive belts, Drive chains, cables, etc.		
	III	• Abnormal phenomena	Unusual noise, overheating, vibration, strange smells, discoloration, incorrect pressure, etc.		
	IV	• Adhesion	Accumulation of debris, peeling, malfunction, etc.		
	V	• Contamination; Damage	Light powder, accumulation of dirt, rust, grease, oil; impact areas, dents, scratches, scuffs, etc.		
			Minor Flaws: Category Subtotal: **Score: divided by 5**		
UNFULFILLED BASIC CONDITIONS	VI	• Lubrication	Insufficient lubrication, dirty oil, undetermined liquid, or leaking lubricant, etc.		
	VII	• Lubricant supply	Lubricant inlets; dirty, damaged, or deformed, faulty pipes, etc.		
	VIII	• Oil level guages	Dirty, leaking, or damaged, no measurement of correct level, etc.		
	IX	• Tightening	Fasteners; nuts, bolts; loose, missing, cross-threaded, crushed, corroded, etc.		
			Unfulfilled Basic Conditions: Category Subtotal: **Score: divided by 4**		
INACCESSIBLE PLACES	X	• Cleaning	Machine, covers, space, layout of machine, space to be able to clean, etc.		
	XI	• Checking	Able to check, layout, instrument location, position and orientation, operating-range known, etc.		
	XII	• Lubricating	Location and position of lubricant nipples, height, lubricant outlet, enough space, etc.		
	XIII	• Operation	Machine layout; position of valves, switches and levers, etc.		
	XIV	• Adjustment	For adjustment, position of gauges, thermometers, flow-meters, moisture and vacuum gauges, etc.		
			Inaccessible Places: Category Subtotal: **Score: divided by 5**		
CONTAMINATION SOURCES	XV	• Product, Raw material	Leaks from products, spilling and mixing product type; Scattered material, too much material, etc.		
	XVI	• Lubricants	Mixing with product, leaks causing contamination, seeping oils, fluids, etc.		
	XVII	• Gases	Lack of pressure, leaking air, gases, steam, vapors, exhaust fumes, etc.		
	XVIII	• Liquids	Leaking waste liquids, not cleaning with solvents, contaminates not out of fluids, etc.		
	XIX	• Scrap, Other	Dunnage, cuttings, non-conforming parts, contaminants by people, forklifts, etc.		
			Contamination Sources: Category Subtotal: **Score: divided by 5**		
QUALITY DEFECT SOURCES	XX	• Moisture	Moisture source, too much, too little, infiltration, temperature change, humidity change, etc.		
	XXI	• Grain size	Right sized filters, old filters, defective filters, operation not considered, etc.		
	XXII	• Concentration, Viscosity	Inadequate acclimation, pre-heating, compounding; Mixing, evaporation, accumulation, stirring, etc.		
	XXIII	• Foreign matter, Shock	Inclusion, entrant of contaminants, chips, scraps; Dropping, jolting, collision, vibration, etc.		
			Quality Defect Sources: Category Subtotal: **Score: divided by 4**		
UNNECESSARY AND NON-URGENT ITEMS	XXIV	• Machinery	Evaluate the hydraulic pumps, their fans, compressors, support columns, tanks, etc.		
	XXV	• Piping equipment	Address pipes, hoses, ducts, valves, dampers, etc.		
	XXVI	• Measuring instruments	Temperatures, pressure gauges, vacuum gauges, amp-meters, etc.		
	XXVII	• Electrical equipment	Wiring, piping, power leads, switches, plugs, etc.		
	XXVIII	• Jigs and tools	General tools, cutting tools, jigs, molds, dies, frames, etc.		
			Unnecessary and Non-urgent Items: Category Subtotal: **Score: divided by 5**		
UNSAFE PLACES	XXIX	• Floors	Cracks, uneven floors, objects, peeling of material, etc.		
	XXX	• Steps	No slip, no handrails, irregular, uneven, too thin, slippery, etc.		
	XXXI	• Lights	Lack of lighting, no protection, dusty and grimy covers, missing lights, etc.		
	XXXII	• Rotating machinery	No protective covers, safety lines, safety cages, no emergency stops, etc.		
	XXXIII	• Lifting gear, Other	Location of hazards, wires, nail heads, split corners, other parts; Solvents, toxic gases, danger signs.		
			Unsafe Places: Category Subtotal: **Score: divided by 5**		**Total "Category Subtotals" Divided by 33 Score: TOTAL**

Abnormality Assessment Form

Date: _____ Evaluation Area: _____

Abnormality	Number	Evaluation Criteria	Rank these items from 1 through 5: 5 being well done	Score (1-5)	Ideas / Suggestions / Comments
MINOR FLAWS	I	• Damage	Cracking, crushing, deformation, chipping, bending, etc.		
	II	• Play, Slackness	Movement, falling out, tilting, eccentricity, distortion, corrosion; Drive belts, Drive chains, cables, etc.		
	III	• Abnormal phenomena	Unusual noise, overheating, vibration, strange smells, discoloration, incorrect pressure, etc.		
	IV	• Adhesion	Accumulation of debris, peeling, malfunction, etc.		
	V	• Contamination; Damage	Light powder, accumulation of dirt, rust, grease, oil; impact areas, dents, scratches, scuffs, etc.		
			Minor Flaws: Category Subtotal:	Score: divided by 5	
UNFULFILLED BASIC CONDITIONS	VI	• Lubrication	Insufficient lubrication, dirty oil, undetermined liquid, or leaking lubricant, etc.		
	VII	• Lubricant supply	Lubricant inlets; dirty, damaged, or deformed, faulty pipes, etc.		
	VIII	• Oil level guages	Dirty, leaking, or damaged, no measurement of correct level, etc.		
	IX	• Tightening	Fasteners; nuts, bolts; loose, missing, cross-threaded, crushed, corroded, etc.		
			Unfulfilled Basic Conditions: Category Subtotal:	Score: divided by 4	
INACCESSIBLE PLACES	X	• Cleaning	Machine, covers, space, layout of machine, space to be able to clean, etc.		
	XI	• Checking	Able to check, layout, instrument location, position and orientation, operating-range known, etc.		
	XII	• Lubricating	Location and position of lubricant nipples, height, lubricant outlet, enough space, etc.		
	XIII	• Operation	Machine layout; position of valves, switches and levers, etc.		
	XIV	• Adjustment	For adjustment, position of gauges, thermometers, flow-meters, moisture and vacuum gauges, etc.		
			Inaccessible Places: Category Subtotal:	Score: divided by 5	
CONTAMINATION SOURCES	XV	• Product, Raw material	Leaks from products, spilling and mixing product type; Scattered material, too much material, etc.		
	XVI	• Lubricants	Mixing with product, leaks causing contamination, seeping oils, fluids, etc.		
	XVII	• Gases	Lack of pressure, leaking air, gases, steam, vapors, exhaust fumes, etc.		
	XVIII	• Liquids	Leaking waste liquids, not cleaning with solvents, contaminates not out of fluids, etc.		
	XIX	• Scrap, Other	Dunnage, cuttings, non-conforming parts, contaminants by people, forklifts, etc.		
			Contamination Sources: Category Subtotal:	Score: divided by 5	
QUALITY DEFECT SOURCES	XX	• Moisture	Moisture source, too much, too little, infiltration, temperature change, humidity change, etc.		
	XXI	• Grain size	Right sized filters, old filters, defective filters, operation not considered, etc.		
	XXII	• Concentration, Viscosity	Inadequate acclimation, pre-heating, compounding; Mixing, evaporation, accumulation, stirring, etc.		
	XXIII	• Foreign matter, Shock	Inclusion, entrant of contaminants, chips, scraps; Dropping, jolting, collision, vibration, etc.		
			Quality Defect Sources: Category Subtotal:	Score: divided by 4	
UNNECESSARY AND NON-URGENT ITEMS	XXIV	• Machinery	Evaluate the hydraulic pumps, their fans, compressors, support columns, tanks, etc.		
	XXV	• Piping equipment	Address pipes, hoses, ducts, valves, dampers, etc.		
	XXVI	• Measuring instruments	Temperatures, pressure gauges, vacuum gauges, amp-meters, etc.		
	XXVII	• Electrical equipment	Wiring, piping, power leads, switches, plugs, etc.		
	XXVIII	• Jigs and tools	General tools, cutting tools, jigs, molds, dies, frames, etc.		
			Unnecessary and Non-urgent Items: Category Subtotal:	Score: divided by 5	
UNSAFE PLACES	XXIX	• Floors	Cracks, uneven floors, objects, peeling of material, etc.		
	XXX	• Steps	No slip, no handrails, irregular, uneven, too thin, slippery, etc.		
	XXXI	• Lights	Lack of lighting, no protection, dusty and grimy covers, missing lights, etc.		
	XXXII	• Rotating machinery	No protective covers, safety lines, safety cages, no emergency stops, etc.		
	XXXIII	• Lifting gear, Other	Location of hazards, wires, nail heads, split corners, other parts; Solvents, toxic gases, danger signs.		
			Unsafe Places: Category Subtotal:	Score: divided by 5	

Total "Category Subtotals" Divided by 33 Score: TOTAL

Abnormality Assessment Form

Date: _____   Evaluation Area: _____

Abnormality	Number	Evaluation Criteria	Rank these items from 1 through 5: 5 being well done	Score (1-5)	Ideas / Suggestions / Comments
MINOR FLAWS	I	• Damage	Cracking, crushing, deformation, chipping, bending, etc.		
	II	• Play, Slackness	Movement, falling out, tilting, eccentricity, distortion, corrosion; Drive belts, Drive chains, cables, etc.		
	III	• Abnormal phenomena	Unusual noise, overheating, vibration, strange smells, discoloration, incorrect pressure, etc.		
	IV	• Adhesion	Accumulation of debris, peeling, malfunction, etc.		
	V	• Contamination; Damage	Light powder, accumulation of dirt, rust, grease, oil; impact areas, dents, scratches, scuffs, etc.		
			Minor Flaws: Category Subtotal: ┊ **Score: divided by 5**		
UNFULFILLED BASIC CONDITIONS	VI	• Lubrication	Insufficient lubrication, dirty oil, undetermined liquid, or leaking lubricant, etc.		
	VII	• Lubricant supply	Lubricant inlets; dirty, damaged, or deformed, faulty pipes, etc.		
	VIII	• Oil level guages	Dirty, leaking, or damaged, no measurement of correct level, etc.		
	IX	• Tightening	Fasteners; nuts, bolts; loose, missing, cross-threaded, crushed, corroded, etc.		
			Unfulfilled Basic Conditions: Category Subtotal: ┊ **Score: divided by 4**		
INACCESSIBLE PLACES	X	• Cleaning	Machine, covers, space, layout of machine, space to be able to clean, etc.		
	XI	• Checking	Able to check, layout, instrument location, position and orientation, operating-range known, etc.		
	XII	• Lubricating	Location and position of lubricant nipples, height, lubricant outlet, enough space, etc.		
	XIII	• Operation	Machine layout; position of valves, switches and levers, etc.		
	XIV	• Adjustment	For adjustment, position of gauges, thermometers, flow-meters, moisture and vacuum gauges, etc.		
			Inaccessible Places: Category Subtotal: ┊ **Score: divided by 5**		
CONTAMINATION SOURCES	XV	• Product, Raw material	Leaks from products, spilling and mixing product type; Scattered material, too much material, etc.		
	XVI	• Lubricants	Mixing with product, leaks causing contamination, seeping oils, fluids, etc.		
	XVII	• Gases	Lack of pressure, leaking air, gases, steam, vapors, exhaust fumes, etc.		
	XVIII	• Liquids	Leaking waste liquids, not cleaning with solvents, contaminates not out of fluids, etc.		
	XIX	• Scrap, Other	Dunnage, cuttings, non-conforming parts, contaminants by people, forklifts, etc.		
			Contamination Sources: Category Subtotal: ┊ **Score: divided by 5**		
QUALITY DEFECT SOURCES	XX	• Moisture	Moisture source, too much, too little, infiltration, temperature change, humidity change, etc.		
	XXI	• Grain size	Right sized filters, old filters, defective filters, operation not considered, etc.		
	XXII	• Concentration, Viscosity	Inadequate acclimation, pre-heating, compounding; Mixing, evaporation, accumulation, stirring, etc.		
	XXIII	• Foreign matter, Shock	Inclusion, entrant of contaminants, chips, scraps; Dropping, jolting, collision, vibration, etc.		
			Quality Defect Sources: Category Subtotal: ┊ **Score: divided by 4**		
UNNECESSARY AND NON-URGENT ITEMS	XXIV	• Machinery	Evaluate the hydraulic pumps, their fans, compressors, support columns, tanks, etc.		
	XXV	• Piping equipment	Address pipes, hoses, ducts, valves, dampers, etc.		
	XXVI	• Measuring instruments	Temperatures, pressure gauges, vacuum gauges, amp-meters, etc.		
	XXVII	• Electrical equipment	Wiring, piping, power leads, switches, plugs, etc.		
	XXVIII	• Jigs and tools	General tools, cutting tools, jigs, molds, dies, frames, etc.		
			Unnecessary and Non-urgent Items: Category Subtotal: ┊ **Score: divided by 5**		
UNSAFE PLACES	XXIX	• Floors	Cracks, uneven floors, objects, peeling of material, etc.		
	XXX	• Steps	No slip, no handrails, irregular, uneven, too thin, slippery, etc.		
	XXXI	• Lights	Lack of lighting, no protection, dusty and grimy covers, missing lights, etc.		
	XXXII	• Rotating machinery	No protective covers, safety lines, safety cages, no emergency stops, etc.		
	XXXIII	• Lifting gear, Other	Location of hazards, wires, nail heads, split corners, other parts; Solvents, toxic gases, danger signs.		
			Unsafe Places: Category Subtotal: ┊ **Score: divided by 5**		

© ENNA
KNOWLEDGE INTO PRACTICE
www.enna.com
www.productivitypress.com

Total "Category Subtotals" Divided by 33 Score: TOTAL

Abnormality Assessment Form

Date: _____   Evaluation Area: _____

Abnormality	Number	Evaluation Criteria	Rank these items from 1 through 5: 5 being well done	Score (1-5)	Ideas / Suggestions / Comments
MINOR FLAWS	I	• Damage	Cracking, crushing, deformation, chipping, bending, etc.		
	II	• Play, Slackness	Movement, falling out, tilting, eccentricity, distortion, corrosion; Drive belts, Drive chains, cables, etc.		
	III	• Abnormal phenomena	Unusual noise, overheating, vibration, strange smells, discoloration, incorrect pressure, etc.		
	IV	• Adhesion	Accumulation of debris, peeling, malfunction, etc.		
	V	• Contamination; Damage	Light powder, accumulation of dirt, rust, grease, oil; impact areas, dents, scratches, scuffs, etc.		
			Minor Flaws: Category Subtotal: ⋮ Score: divided by 5		
UNFULFILLED BASIC CONDITIONS	VI	• Lubrication	Insufficient lubrication, dirty oil, undetermined liquid, or leaking lubricant, etc.		
	VII	• Lubricant supply	Lubricant inlets; dirty, damaged, or deformed, faulty pipes, etc.		
	VIII	• Oil level guages	Dirty, leaking, or damaged, no measurement of correct level, etc.		
	IX	• Tightening	Fasteners; nuts, bolts; loose, missing, cross-threaded, crushed, corroded, etc.		
			Unfulfilled Basic Conditions: Category Subtotal: ⋮ Score: divided by 4		
INACCESSIBLE PLACES	X	• Cleaning	Machine, covers, space, layout of machine, space to be able to clean, etc.		
	XI	• Checking	Able to check, layout, instrument location, position and orientation, operating-range known, etc.		
	XII	• Lubricating	Location and position of lubricant nipples, height, lubricant outlet, enough space, etc.		
	XIII	• Operation	Machine layout; position of valves, switches and levers, etc.		
	XIV	• Adjustment	For adjustment, position of gauges, thermometers, flow-meters, moisture and vacuum gauges, etc.		
			Inaccessible Places: Category Subtotal: ⋮ Score: divided by 5		
CONTAMINATION SOURCES	XV	• Product, Raw material	Leaks from products, spilling and mixing product type; Scattered material, too much material, etc.		
	XVI	• Lubricants	Mixing with product, leaks causing contamination, seeping oils, fluids, etc.		
	XVII	• Gases	Lack of pressure, leaking air, gases, steam, vapors, exhaust fumes, etc.		
	XVIII	• Liquids	Leaking waste liquids, not cleaning with solvents, contaminates not out of fluids, etc.		
	XIX	• Scrap, Other	Dunnage, cuttings, non-conforming parts, contaminants by people, forklifts, etc.		
			Contamination Sources: Category Subtotal: ⋮ Score: divided by 5		
QUALITY DEFECT SOURCES	XX	• Moisture	Moisture source, too much, too little, infiltration, temperature change, humidity change, etc.		
	XXI	• Grain size	Right sized filters, old filters, defective filters, operation not considered, etc.		
	XXII	• Concentration, Viscosity	Inadequate acclimation, pre-heating, compounding; Mixing, evaporation, accumulation, stirring, etc.		
	XXIII	• Foreign matter, Shock	Inclusion, entrant of contaminants, chips, scraps; Dropping, jolting, collision, vibration, etc.		
			Quality Defect Sources: Category Subtotal: ⋮ Score: divided by 4		
UNNECESSARY AND NON-URGENT ITEMS	XXIV	• Machinery	Evaluate the hydraulic pumps, their fans, compressors, support columns, tanks, etc.		
	XXV	• Piping equipment	Address pipes, hoses, ducts, valves, dampers, etc.		
	XXVI	• Measuring instruments	Temperatures, pressure gauges, vacuum gauges, amp-meters, etc.		
	XXVII	• Electrical equipment	Wiring, piping, power leads, switches, plugs, etc.		
	XXVIII	• Jigs and tools	General tools, cutting tools, jigs, molds, dies, frames, etc.		
			Unnecessary and Non-urgent Items: Category Subtotal: ⋮ Score: divided by 5		
UNSAFE PLACES	XXIX	• Floors	Cracks, uneven floors, objects, peeling of material, etc.		
	XXX	• Steps	No slip, no handrails, irregular, uneven, too thin, slippery, etc.		
	XXXI	• Lights	Lack of lighting, no protection, dusty and grimy covers, missing lights, etc.		
	XXXII	• Rotating machinery	No protective covers, safety lines, safety cages, no emergency stops, etc.		
	XXXIII	• Lifting gear, Other	Location of hazards, wires, nail heads, split corners, other parts; Solvents, toxic gases, danger signs.		
			Unsafe Places: Category Subtotal: ⋮ Score: divided by 5		

© ENNA
KNOWLEDGE INTO PRACTICE
www.enna.com
www.productivitypress.com

Total "Category Subtotals" Divided by 33 Score: TOTAL ┆

Abnormality Assessment Form

Date: _____   Evaluation Area: _____

Abnormality	Number	Evaluation Criteria	Rank these items from 1 through 5: 5 being well done	Score (1-5)	Ideas / Suggestions / Comments
MINOR FLAWS	I	• Damage	Cracking, crushing, deformation, chipping, bending, etc.		
	II	• Play, Slackness	Movement, falling out, tilting, eccentricity, distortion, corrosion; Drive belts, Drive chains, cables, etc.		
	III	• Abnormal phenomena	Unusual noise, overheating, vibration, strange smells, discoloration, incorrect pressure, etc.		
	IV	• Adhesion	Accumulation of debris, peeling, malfunction, etc.		
	V	• Contamination; Damage	Light powder, accumulation of dirt, rust, grease, oil; impact areas, dents, scratches, scuffs, etc.		
			Minor Flaws: Category Subtotal:	Score: divided by 5	
UNFULFILLED BASIC CONDITIONS	VI	• Lubrication	Insufficient lubrication, dirty oil, undetermined liquid, or leaking lubricant, etc.		
	VII	• Lubricant supply	Lubricant inlets; dirty, damaged, or deformed, faulty pipes, etc.		
	VIII	• Oil level guages	Dirty, leaking, or damaged, no measurement of correct level, etc.		
	IX	• Tightening	Fasteners; nuts, bolts; loose, missing, cross-threaded, crushed, corroded, etc.		
			Unfulfilled Basic Conditions: Category Subtotal:	Score: divided by 4	
INACCESSIBLE PLACES	X	• Cleaning	Machine, covers, space, layout of machine, space to be able to clean, etc.		
	XI	• Checking	Able to check, layout, instrument location, position and orientation, operating-range known, etc.		
	XII	• Lubricating	Location and position of lubricant nipples, height, lubricant outlet, enough space, etc.		
	XIII	• Operation	Machine layout; position of valves, switches and levers, etc.		
	XIV	• Adjustment	For adjustment, position of gauges, thermometers, flow-meters, moisture and vacuum gauges, etc.		
			Inaccessible Places: Category Subtotal:	Score: divided by 5	
CONTAMINATION SOURCES	XV	• Product, Raw material	Leaks from products, spilling and mixing product type; Scattered material, too much material, etc.		
	XVI	• Lubricants	Mixing with product, leaks causing contamination, seeping oils, fluids, etc.		
	XVII	• Gases	Lack of pressure, leaking air, gases, steam, vapors, exhaust fumes, etc.		
	XVIII	• Liquids	Leaking waste liquids, not cleaning with solvents, contaminates not out of fluids, etc.		
	XIX	• Scrap, Other	Dunnage, cuttings, non-conforming parts, contaminants by people, forklifts, etc.		
			Contamination Sources: Category Subtotal:	Score: divided by 5	
QUALITY DEFECT SOURCES	XX	• Moisture	Moisture source, too much, too little, infiltration, temperature change, humidity change, etc.		
	XXI	• Grain size	Right sized filters, old filters, defective filters, operation not considered, etc.		
	XXII	• Concentration, Viscosity	Inadequate acclimation, pre-heating, compounding; Mixing, evaporation, accumulation, stirring, etc.		
	XXIII	• Foreign matter, Shock	Inclusion, entrant of contaminants, chips, scraps; Dropping, jolting, collision, vibration, etc.		
			Quality Defect Sources: Category Subtotal:	Score: divided by 4	
UNNECESSARY AND NON-URGENT ITEMS	XXIV	• Machinery	Evaluate the hydraulic pumps, their fans, compressors, support columns, tanks, etc.		
	XXV	• Piping equipment	Address pipes, hoses, ducts, valves, dampers, etc.		
	XXVI	• Measuring instruments	Temperatures, pressure gauges, vacuum gauges, amp-meters, etc.		
	XXVII	• Electrical equipment	Wiring, piping, power leads, switches, plugs, etc.		
	XXVIII	• Jigs and tools	General tools, cutting tools, jigs, molds, dies, frames, etc.		
			Unnecessary and Non-urgent Items: Category Subtotal:	Score: divided by 5	
UNSAFE PLACES	XXIX	• Floors	Cracks, uneven floors, objects, peeling of material, etc.		
	XXX	• Steps	No slip, no handrails, irregular, uneven, too thin, slippery, etc.		
	XXXI	• Lights	Lack of lighting, no protection, dusty and grimy covers, missing lights, etc.		
	XXXII	• Rotating machinery	No protective covers, safety lines, safety cages, no emergency stops, etc.		
	XXXIII	• Lifting gear, Other	Location of hazards, wires, nail heads, split corners, other parts; Solvents, toxic gases, danger signs.		
			Unsafe Places: Category Subtotal:	Score: divided by 5	**Total "Category Subtotals" Divided by 33 Score: TOTAL**

www.enna.com
www.productivitypress.com

Abnormality Assessment Form

Date: _____   Evaluation Area: _____

Abnormality	Number	Evaluation Criteria	Rank these items from 1 through 5: 5 being well done	Score (1-5)	Ideas / Suggestions / Comments
MINOR FLAWS	I	• Damage	Cracking, crushing, deformation, chipping, bending, etc.		
	II	• Play, Slackness	Movement, falling out, tilting, eccentricity, distortion, corrosion; Drive belts, Drive chains, cables, etc.		
	III	• Abnormal phenomena	Unusual noise, overheating, vibration, strange smells, discoloration, incorrect pressure, etc.		
	IV	• Adhesion	Accumulation of debris, peeling, malfunction, etc.		
	V	• Contamination; Damage	Light powder, accumulation of dirt, rust, grease, oil; impact areas, dents, scratches, scuffs, etc.		
			Minor Flaws: Category Subtotal:	Score: divided by 5	
UNFULFILLED BASIC CONDITIONS	VI	• Lubrication	Insufficient lubrication, dirty oil, undetermined liquid, or leaking lubricant, etc.		
	VII	• Lubricant supply	Lubricant inlets; dirty, damaged, or deformed, faulty pipes, etc.		
	VIII	• Oil level guages	Dirty, leaking, or damaged, no measurement of correct level, etc.		
	IX	• Tightening	Fasteners; nuts, bolts; loose, missing, cross-threaded, crushed, corroded, etc.		
			Unfulfilled Basic Conditions: Category Subtotal:	Score: divided by 4	
INACCESSIBLE PLACES	X	• Cleaning	Machine, covers, space, layout of machine, space to be able to clean, etc.		
	XI	• Checking	Able to check, layout, instrument location, position and orientation, operating-range known, etc.		
	XII	• Lubricating	Location and position of lubricant nipples, height, lubricant outlet, enough space, etc.		
	XIII	• Operation	Machine layout; position of valves, switches and levers, etc.		
	XIV	• Adjustment	For adjustment, position of gauges, thermometers, flow-meters, moisture and vacuum gauges, etc.		
			Inaccessible Places: Category Subtotal:	Score: divided by 5	
CONTAMINATION SOURCES	XV	• Product, Raw material	Leaks from products, spilling and mixing product type; Scattered material, too much material, etc.		
	XVI	• Lubricants	Mixing with product, leaks causing contamination, seeping oils, fluids, etc.		
	XVII	• Gases	Lack of pressure, leaking air, gases, steam, vapors, exhaust fumes, etc.		
	XVIII	• Liquids	Leaking waste liquids, not cleaning with solvents, contaminates not out of fluids, etc.		
	XIX	• Scrap, Other	Dunnage, cuttings, non-conforming parts, contaminants by people, forklifts, etc.		
			Contamination Sources: Category Subtotal:	Score: divided by 5	
QUALITY DEFECT SOURCES	XX	• Moisture	Moisture source, too much, too little, infiltration, temperature change, humidity change, etc.		
	XXI	• Grain size	Right sized filters, old filters, defective filters, operation not considered, etc.		
	XXII	• Concentration, Viscosity	Inadequate acclimation, pre-heating, compounding; Mixing, evaporation, accumulation, stirring, etc.		
	XXIII	• Foreign matter, Shock	Inclusion, entrant of contaminants, chips, scraps; Dropping, jolting, collision, vibration, etc.		
			Quality Defect Sources: Category Subtotal:	Score: divided by 4	
UNNECESSARY AND NON-URGENT ITEMS	XXIV	• Machinery	Evaluate the hydraulic pumps, their fans, compressors, support columns, tanks, etc.		
	XXV	• Piping equipment	Address pipes, hoses, ducts, valves, dampers, etc.		
	XXVI	• Measuring instruments	Temperatures, pressure gauges, vacuum gauges, amp-meters, etc.		
	XXVII	• Electrical equipment	Wiring, piping, power leads, switches, plugs, etc.		
	XXVIII	• Jigs and tools	General tools, cutting tools, jigs, molds, dies, frames, etc.		
			Unnecessary and Non-urgent Items: Category Subtotal:	Score: divided by 5	
UNSAFE PLACES	XXIX	• Floors	Cracks, uneven floors, objects, peeling of material, etc.		
	XXX	• Steps	No slip, no handrails, irregular, uneven, too thin, slippery, etc.		
	XXXI	• Lights	Lack of lighting, no protection, dusty and grimy covers, missing lights, etc.		
	XXXII	• Rotating machinery	No protective covers, safety lines, safety cages, no emergency stops, etc.		
	XXXIII	• Lifting gear, Other	Location of hazards, wires, nail heads, split corners, other parts; Solvents, toxic gases, danger signs.		
			Unsafe Places: Category Subtotal:	Score: divided by 5	

Total "Category Subtotals" Divided by 33 Score: TOTAL

Abnormality Assessment Form

Date: _____ Evaluation Area: _____

Abnormality	Number	Evaluation Criteria	Rank these items from 1 through 5: 5 being well done	Score (1-5)	Ideas / Suggestions / Comments
MINOR FLAWS	I	• Damage	Cracking, crushing, deformation, chipping, bending, etc.		
	II	• Play, Slackness	Movement, falling out, tilting, eccentricity, distortion, corrosion; Drive belts, Drive chains, cables, etc.		
	III	• Abnormal phenomena	Unusual noise, overheating, vibration, strange smells, discoloration, incorrect pressure, etc.		
	IV	• Adhesion	Accumulation of debris, peeling, malfunction, etc.		
	V	• Contamination; Damage	Light powder, accumulation of dirt, rust, grease, oil; impact areas, dents, scratches, scuffs, etc.		
			Minor Flaws: Category Subtotal:	Score: divided by 5	
UNFULFILLED BASIC CONDITIONS	VI	• Lubrication	Insufficient lubrication, dirty oil, undetermined liquid, or leaking lubricant, etc.		
	VII	• Lubricant supply	Lubricant inlets; dirty, damaged, or deformed, faulty pipes, etc.		
	VIII	• Oil level guages	Dirty, leaking, or damaged, no measurement of correct level, etc.		
	IX	• Tightening	Fasteners; nuts, bolts; loose, missing, cross-threaded, crushed, corroded, etc.		
			Unfulfilled Basic Conditions: Category Subtotal:	Score: divided by 4	
INACCESSIBLE PLACES	X	• Cleaning	Machine, covers, space, layout of machine, space to be able to clean, etc.		
	XI	• Checking	Able to check, layout, instrument location, position and orientation, operating-range known, etc.		
	XII	• Lubricating	Location and position of lubricant nipples, height, lubricant outlet, enough space, etc.		
	XIII	• Operation	Machine layout; position of valves, switches and levers, etc.		
	XIV	• Adjustment	For adjustment, position of gauges, thermometers, flow-meters, moisture and vacuum gauges, etc.		
			Inaccessible Places: Category Subtotal:	Score: divided by 5	
CONTAMINATION SOURCES	XV	• Product, Raw material	Leaks from products, spilling and mixing product type; Scattered material, too much material, etc.		
	XVI	• Lubricants	Mixing with product, leaks causing contamination, seeping oils, fluids, etc.		
	XVII	• Gases	Lack of pressure, leaking air, gases, steam, vapors, exhaust fumes, etc.		
	XVIII	• Liquids	Leaking waste liquids, not cleaning with solvents, contaminates not out of fluids, etc.		
	XIX	• Scrap, Other	Dunnage, cuttings, non-conforming parts, contaminants by people, forklifts, etc.		
			Contamination Sources: Category Subtotal:	Score: divided by 5	
QUALITY DEFECT SOURCES	XX	• Moisture	Moisture source, too much, too little, infiltration, temperature change, humidity change, etc.		
	XXI	• Grain size	Right sized filters, old filters, defective filters, operation not considered, etc.		
	XXII	• Concentration, Viscosity	Inadequate acclimation, pre-heating, compounding; Mixing, evaporation, accumulation, stirring, etc.		
	XXIII	• Foreign matter, Shock	Inclusion, entrant of contaminants, chips, scraps; Dropping, jolting, collision, vibration, etc.		
			Quality Defect Sources: Category Subtotal:	Score: divided by 4	
UNNECESSARY AND NON-URGENT ITEMS	XXIV	• Machinery	Evaluate the hydraulic pumps, their fans, compressors, support columns, tanks, etc.		
	XXV	• Piping equipment	Address pipes, hoses, ducts, valves, dampers, etc.		
	XXVI	• Measuring instruments	Temperatures, pressure gauges, vacuum gauges, amp-meters, etc.		
	XXVII	• Electrical equipment	Wiring, piping, power leads, switches, plugs, etc.		
	XXVIII	• Jigs and tools	General tools, cutting tools, jigs, molds, dies, frames, etc.		
			Unnecessary and Non-urgent Items: Category Subtotal:	Score: divided by 5	
UNSAFE PLACES	XXIX	• Floors	Cracks, uneven floors, objects, peeling of material, etc.		
	XXX	• Steps	No slip, no handrails, irregular, uneven, too thin, slippery, etc.		
	XXXI	• Lights	Lack of lighting, no protection, dusty and grimy covers, missing lights, etc.		
	XXXII	• Rotating machinery	No protective covers, safety lines, safety cages, no emergency stops, etc.		
	XXXIII	• Lifting gear, Other	Location of hazards, wires, nail heads, split corners, other parts; Solvents, toxic gases, danger signs.		
			Unsafe Places: Category Subtotal:	Score: divided by 5	

Total "Category Subtotals" Divided by 33 Score: TOTAL

Abnormality Assessment Form

Date: _____   Evaluation Area: _____

Abnormality	Number	Evaluation Criteria	Rank these items from 1 through 5: 5 being well done	Score (1-5)	Ideas / Suggestions / Comments
MINOR FLAWS	I	• Damage	Cracking, crushing, deformation, chipping, bending, etc.		
	II	• Play, Slackness	Movement, falling out, tilting, eccentricity, distortion, corrosion; Drive belts, Drive chains, cables, etc.		
	III	• Abnormal phenomena	Unusual noise, overheating, vibration, strange smells, discoloration, incorrect pressure, etc.		
	IV	• Adhesion	Accumulation of debris, peeling, malfunction, etc.		
	V	• Contamination; Damage	Light powder, accumulation of dirt, rust, grease, oil; impact areas, dents, scratches, scuffs, etc.		
			Minor Flaws: Category Subtotal:	Score: divided by 5	
UNFULFILLED BASIC CONDITIONS	VI	• Lubrication	Insufficient lubrication, dirty oil, undetermined liquid, or leaking lubricant, etc.		
	VII	• Lubricant supply	Lubricant inlets; dirty, damaged, or deformed, faulty pipes, etc.		
	VIII	• Oil level guages	Dirty, leaking, or damaged, no measurement of correct level, etc.		
	IX	• Tightening	Fasteners; nuts, bolts; loose, missing, cross-threaded, crushed, corroded, etc.		
			Unfulfilled Basic Conditions: Category Subtotal:	Score: divided by 4	
INACCESSIBLE PLACES	X	• Cleaning	Machine, covers, space, layout of machine, space to be able to clean, etc.		
	XI	• Checking	Able to check, layout, instrument location, position and orientation, operating-range known, etc.		
	XII	• Lubricating	Location and position of lubricant nipples, height, lubricant outlet, enough space, etc.		
	XIII	• Operation	Machine layout; position of valves, switches and levers, etc.		
	XIV	• Adjustment	For adjustment, position of gauges, thermometers, flow-meters, moisture and vacuum gauges, etc.		
			Inaccessible Places: Category Subtotal:	Score: divided by 5	
CONTAMINATION SOURCES	XV	• Product, Raw material	Leaks from products, spilling and mixing product type; Scattered material, too much material, etc.		
	XVI	• Lubricants	Mixing with product, leaks causing contamination, seeping oils, fluids, etc.		
	XVII	• Gases	Lack of pressure, leaking air, gases, steam, vapors, exhaust fumes, etc.		
	XVIII	• Liquids	Leaking waste liquids, not cleaning with solvents, contaminates not out of fluids, etc.		
	XIX	• Scrap, Other	Dunnage, cuttings, non-conforming parts, contaminants by people, forklifts, etc.		
			Contamination Sources: Category Subtotal:	Score: divided by 5	
QUALITY DEFECT SOURCES	XX	• Moisture	Moisture source, too much, too little, infiltration, temperature change, humidity change, etc.		
	XXI	• Grain size	Right sized filters, old filters, defective filters, operation not considered, etc.		
	XXII	• Concentration, Viscosity	Inadequate acclimation, pre-heating, compounding; Mixing, evaporation, accumulation, stirring, etc.		
	XXIII	• Foreign matter, Shock	Inclusion, entrant of contaminants, chips, scraps; Dropping, jolting, collision, vibration, etc.		
			Quality Defect Sources: Category Subtotal:	Score: divided by 4	
UNNECESSARY AND NON-URGENT ITEMS	XXIV	• Machinery	Evaluate the hydraulic pumps, their fans, compressors, support columns, tanks, etc.		
	XXV	• Piping equipment	Address pipes, hoses, ducts, valves, dampers, etc.		
	XXVI	• Measuring instruments	Temperatures, pressure gauges, vacuum gauges, amp-meters, etc.		
	XXVII	• Electrical equipment	Wiring, piping, power leads, switches, plugs, etc.		
	XXVIII	• Jigs and tools	General tools, cutting tools, jigs, molds, dies, frames, etc.		
			Unnecessary and Non-urgent Items: Category Subtotal:	Score: divided by 5	
UNSAFE PLACES	XXIX	• Floors	Cracks, uneven floors, objects, peeling of material, etc.		
	XXX	• Steps	No slip, no handrails, irregular, uneven, too thin, slippery, etc.		
	XXXI	• Lights	Lack of lighting, no protection, dusty and grimy covers, missing lights, etc.		
	XXXII	• Rotating machinery	No protective covers, safety lines, safety cages, no emergency stops, etc.		
	XXXIII	• Lifting gear, Other	Location of hazards, wires, nail heads, split corners, other parts; Solvents, toxic gases, danger signs.		
			Unsafe Places: Category Subtotal:	Score: divided by 5	

Total "Category Subtotals" Divided by 33 Score: TOTAL

Abnormality Assessment Form

Date: _____   Evaluation Area: _____

Abnormality	Number	Evaluation Criteria	Rank these items from 1 through 5: 5 being well done	Score (1-5)	Ideas / Suggestions / Comments
MINOR FLAWS	I	• Damage	Cracking, crushing, deformation, chipping, bending, etc.		
	II	• Play, Slackness	Movement, falling out, tilting, eccentricity, distortion, corrosion; Drive belts, Drive chains, cables, etc.		
	III	• Abnormal phenomena	Unusual noise, overheating, vibration, strange smells, discoloration, incorrect pressure, etc.		
	IV	• Adhesion	Accumulation of debris, peeling, malfunction, etc.		
	V	• Contamination; Damage	Light powder, accumulation of dirt, rust, grease, oil; impact areas, dents, scratches, scuffs, etc.		
			Minor Flaws: Category Subtotal: Score: divided by 5		
UNFULFILLED BASIC CONDITIONS	VI	• Lubrication	Insufficient lubrication, dirty oil, undetermined liquid, or leaking lubricant, etc.		
	VII	• Lubricant supply	Lubricant inlets; dirty, damaged, or deformed, faulty pipes, etc.		
	VIII	• Oil level guages	Dirty, leaking, or damaged, no measurement of correct level, etc.		
	IX	• Tightening	Fasteners; nuts, bolts; loose, missing, cross-threaded, crushed, corroded, etc.		
			Unfulfilled Basic Conditions: Category Subtotal: Score: divided by 4		
INACCESSIBLE PLACES	X	• Cleaning	Machine, covers, space, layout of machine, space to be able to clean, etc.		
	XI	• Checking	Able to check, layout, instrument location, position and orientation, operating-range known, etc.		
	XII	• Lubricating	Location and position of lubricant nipples, height, lubricant outlet, enough space, etc.		
	XIII	• Operation	Machine layout; position of valves, switches and levers, etc.		
	XIV	• Adjustment	For adjustment, position of gauges, thermometers, flow-meters, moisture and vacuum gauges, etc.		
			Inaccessible Places: Category Subtotal: Score: divided by 5		
CONTAMINATION SOURCES	XV	• Product, Raw material	Leaks from products, spilling and mixing product type; Scattered material, too much material, etc.		
	XVI	• Lubricants	Mixing with product, leaks causing contamination, seeping oils, fluids, etc.		
	XVII	• Gases	Lack of pressure, leaking air, gases, steam, vapors, exhaust fumes, etc.		
	XVIII	• Liquids	Leaking waste liquids, not cleaning with solvents, contaminates not out of fluids, etc.		
	XIX	• Scrap, Other	Dunnage, cuttings, non-conforming parts, contaminants by people, forklifts, etc.		
			Contamination Sources: Category Subtotal: Score: divided by 5		
QUALITY DEFECT SOURCES	XX	• Moisture	Moisture source, too much, too little, infiltration, temperature change, humidity change, etc.		
	XXI	• Grain size	Right sized filters, old filters, defective filters, operation not considered, etc.		
	XXII	• Concentration, Viscosity	Inadequate acclimation, pre-heating, compounding; Mixing, evaporation, accumulation, stirring, etc.		
	XXIII	• Foreign matter, Shock	Inclusion, entrant of contaminants, chips, scraps; Dropping, jolting, collision, vibration, etc.		
			Quality Defect Sources: Category Subtotal: Score: divided by 4		
UNNECESSARY AND NON-URGENT ITEMS	XXIV	• Machinery	Evaluate the hydraulic pumps, their fans, compressors, support columns, tanks, etc.		
	XXV	• Piping equipment	Address pipes, hoses, ducts, valves, dampers, etc.		
	XXVI	• Measuring instruments	Temperatures, pressure gauges, vacuum gauges, amp-meters, etc.		
	XXVII	• Electrical equipment	Wiring, piping, power leads, switches, plugs, etc.		
	XXVIII	• Jigs and tools	General tools, cutting tools, jigs, molds, dies, frames, etc.		
			Unnecessary and Non-urgent Items: Category Subtotal: Score: divided by 5		
UNSAFE PLACES	XXIX	• Floors	Cracks, uneven floors, objects, peeling of material, etc.		
	XXX	• Steps	No slip, no handrails, irregular, uneven, too thin, slippery, etc.		
	XXXI	• Lights	Lack of lighting, no protection, dusty and grimy covers, missing lights, etc.		
	XXXII	• Rotating machinery	No protective covers, safety lines, safety cages, no emergency stops, etc.		
	XXXIII	• Lifting gear, Other	Location of hazards, wires, nail heads, split corners, other parts; Solvents, toxic gases, danger signs.		
			Unsafe Places: Category Subtotal: Score: divided by 5		

Total "Category Subtotals" Divided by 33 Score: TOTAL

Abnormality Assessment Form

Date: _____   Evaluation Area: _____

Abnormality	Number	Evaluation Criteria	Rank these items from 1 through 5: 5 being well done	Score (1-5)	Ideas / Suggestions / Comments
MINOR FLAWS	I	• Damage	Cracking, crushing, deformation, chipping, bending, etc.		
	II	• Play, Slackness	Movement, falling out, tilting, eccentricity, distortion, corrosion; Drive belts, Drive chains, cables, etc.		
	III	• Abnormal phenomena	Unusual noise, overheating, vibration, strange smells, discoloration, incorrect pressure, etc.		
	IV	• Adhesion	Accumulation of debris, peeling, malfunction, etc.		
	V	• Contamination; Damage	Light powder, accumulation of dirt, rust, grease, oil; impact areas, dents, scratches, scuffs, etc.		
			Minor Flaws: Category Subtotal: Score: divided by 5		
UNFULFILLED BASIC CONDITIONS	VI	• Lubrication	Insufficient lubrication, dirty oil, undetermined liquid, or leaking lubricant, etc.		
	VII	• Lubricant supply	Lubricant inlets; dirty, damaged, or deformed, faulty pipes, etc.		
	VIII	• Oil level guages	Dirty, leaking, or damaged, no measurement of correct level, etc.		
	IX	• Tightening	Fasteners; nuts, bolts; loose, missing, cross-threaded, crushed, corroded, etc.		
			Unfulfilled Basic Conditions: Category Subtotal: Score: divided by 4		
INACCESSIBLE PLACES	X	• Cleaning	Machine, covers, space, layout of machine, space to be able to clean, etc.		
	XI	• Checking	Able to check, layout, instrument location, position and orientation, operating-range known, etc.		
	XII	• Lubricating	Location and position of lubricant nipples, height, lubricant outlet, enough space, etc.		
	XIII	• Operation	Machine layout; position of valves, switches and levers, etc.		
	XIV	• Adjustment	For adjustment, position of gauges, thermometers, flow-meters, moisture and vacuum gauges, etc.		
			Inaccessible Places: Category Subtotal: Score: divided by 5		
CONTAMINATION SOURCES	XV	• Product, Raw material	Leaks from products, spilling and mixing product type; Scattered material, too much material, etc.		
	XVI	• Lubricants	Mixing with product, leaks causing contamination, seeping oils, fluids, etc.		
	XVII	• Gases	Lack of pressure, leaking air, gases, steam, vapors, exhaust fumes, etc.		
	XVIII	• Liquids	Leaking waste liquids, not cleaning with solvents, contaminates not out of fluids, etc.		
	XIX	• Scrap, Other	Dunnage, cuttings, non-conforming parts, contaminants by people, forklifts, etc.		
			Contamination Sources: Category Subtotal: Score: divided by 5		
QUALITY DEFECT SOURCES	XX	• Moisture	Moisture source, too much, too little, infiltration, temperature change, humidity change, etc.		
	XXI	• Grain size	Right sized filters, old filters, defective filters, operation not considered, etc.		
	XXII	• Concentration, Viscosity	Inadequate acclimation, pre-heating, compounding; Mixing, evaporation, accumulation, stirring, etc.		
	XXIII	• Foreign matter, Shock	Inclusion, entrant of contaminants, chips, scraps; Dropping, jolting, collision, vibration, etc.		
			Quality Defect Sources: Category Subtotal: Score: divided by 4		
UNNECESSARY AND NON-URGENT ITEMS	XXIV	• Machinery	Evaluate the hydraulic pumps, their fans, compressors, support columns, tanks, etc.		
	XXV	• Piping equipment	Address pipes, hoses, ducts, valves, dampers, etc.		
	XXVI	• Measuring instruments	Temperatures, pressure gauges, vacuum gauges, amp-meters, etc.		
	XXVII	• Electrical equipment	Wiring, piping, power leads, switches, plugs, etc.		
	XXVIII	• Jigs and tools	General tools, cutting tools, jigs, molds, dies, frames, etc.		
			Unnecessary and Non-urgent Items: Category Subtotal: Score: divided by 5		
UNSAFE PLACES	XXIX	• Floors	Cracks, uneven floors, objects, peeling of material, etc.		
	XXX	• Steps	No slip, no handrails, irregular, uneven, too thin, slippery, etc.		
	XXXI	• Lights	Lack of lighting, no protection, dusty and grimy covers, missing lights, etc.		
	XXXII	• Rotating machinery	No protective covers, safety lines, safety cages, no emergency stops, etc.		
	XXXIII	• Lifting gear, Other	Location of hazards, wires, nail heads, split corners, other parts; Solvents, toxic gases, danger signs.		
			Unsafe Places: Category Subtotal: Score: divided by 5		**Total "Category Subtotals" Divided by 33 Score: TOTAL**

Abnormality Assessment Form

Date: _____ Evaluation Area: _____

Abnormality	Number	Evaluation Criteria	Rank these items from 1 through 5: 5 being well done	Score (1-5)	Ideas / Suggestions / Comments
MINOR FLAWS	I	• Damage	Cracking, crushing, deformation, chipping, bending, etc.		
	II	• Play, Slackness	Movement, falling out, tilting, eccentricity, distortion, corrosion; Drive belts, Drive chains, cables, etc.		
	III	• Abnormal phenomena	Unusual noise, overheating, vibration, strange smells, discoloration, incorrect pressure, etc.		
	IV	• Adhesion	Accumulation of debris, peeling, malfunction, etc.		
	V	• Contamination; Damage	Light powder, accumulation of dirt, rust, grease, oil; impact areas, dents, scratches, scuffs, etc.		
			Minor Flaws: Category Subtotal: Score: divided by 5		
UNFULFILLED BASIC CONDITIONS	VI	• Lubrication	Insufficient lubrication, dirty oil, undetermined liquid, or leaking lubricant, etc.		
	VII	• Lubricant supply	Lubricant inlets; dirty, damaged, or deformed, faulty pipes, etc.		
	VIII	• Oil level guages	Dirty, leaking, or damaged, no measurement of correct level, etc.		
	IX	• Tightening	Fasteners; nuts, bolts; loose, missing, cross-threaded, crushed, corroded, etc.		
			Unfulfilled Basic Conditions: Category Subtotal: Score: divided by 4		
INACCESSIBLE PLACES	X	• Cleaning	Machine, covers, space, layout of machine, space to be able to clean, etc.		
	XI	• Checking	Able to check, layout, instrument location, position and orientation, operating-range known, etc.		
	XII	• Lubricating	Location and position of lubricant nipples, height, lubricant outlet, enough space, etc.		
	XIII	• Operation	Machine layout; position of valves, switches and levers, etc.		
	XIV	• Adjustment	For adjustment, position of gauges, thermometers, flow-meters, moisture and vacuum gauges, etc.		
			Inaccessible Places: Category Subtotal: Score: divided by 5		
CONTAMINATION SOURCES	XV	• Product, Raw material	Leaks from products, spilling and mixing product type; Scattered material, too much material, etc.		
	XVI	• Lubricants	Mixing with product, leaks causing contamination, seeping oils, fluids, etc.		
	XVII	• Gases	Lack of pressure, leaking air, gases, steam, vapors, exhaust fumes, etc.		
	XVIII	• Liquids	Leaking waste liquids, not cleaning with solvents, contaminates not out of fluids, etc.		
	XIX	• Scrap, Other	Dunnage, cuttings, non-conforming parts, contaminants by people, forklifts, etc.		
			Contamination Sources: Category Subtotal: Score: divided by 5		
QUALITY DEFECT SOURCES	XX	• Moisture	Moisture source, too much, too little, infiltration, temperature change, humidity change, etc.		
	XXI	• Grain size	Right sized filters, old filters, defective filters, operation not considered, etc.		
	XXII	• Concentration, Viscosity	Inadequate acclimation, pre-heating, compounding; Mixing, evaporation, accumulation, stirring, etc.		
	XXIII	• Foreign matter, Shock	Inclusion, entrant of contaminants, chips, scraps; Dropping, jolting, collision, vibration, etc.		
			Quality Defect Sources: Category Subtotal: Score: divided by 4		
UNNECESSARY AND NON-URGENT ITEMS	XXIV	• Machinery	Evaluate the hydraulic pumps, their fans, compressors, support columns, tanks, etc.		
	XXV	• Piping equipment	Address pipes, hoses, ducts, valves, dampers, etc.		
	XXVI	• Measuring instruments	Temperatures, pressure gauges, vacuum gauges, amp-meters, etc.		
	XXVII	• Electrical equipment	Wiring, piping, power leads, switches, plugs, etc.		
	XXVIII	• Jigs and tools	General tools, cutting tools, jigs, molds, dies, frames, etc.		
			Unnecessary and Non-urgent Items: Category Subtotal: Score: divided by 5		
UNSAFE PLACES	XXIX	• Floors	Cracks, uneven floors, objects, peeling of material, etc.		
	XXX	• Steps	No slip, no handrails, irregular, uneven, too thin, slippery, etc.		
	XXXI	• Lights	Lack of lighting, no protection, dusty and grimy covers, missing lights, etc.		
	XXXII	• Rotating machinery	No protective covers, safety lines, safety cages, no emergency stops, etc.		
	XXXIII	• Lifting gear, Other	Location of hazards, wires, nail heads, split corners, other parts; Solvents, toxic gases, danger signs.		
			Unsafe Places: Category Subtotal: Score: divided by 5		

Total "Category Subtotals" Divided by 33 Score: TOTAL

Abnormality Assessment Form

Date: _____ Evaluation Area: _____

Abnormality	Number	Evaluation Criteria	Rank these items from 1 through 5: 5 being well done	Score (1-5)	Ideas / Suggestions / Comments
MINOR FLAWS	I	• Damage	Cracking, crushing, deformation, chipping, bending, etc.		
	II	• Play, Slackness	Movement, falling out, tilting, eccentricity, distortion, corrosion; Drive belts, Drive chains, cables, etc.		
	III	• Abnormal phenomena	Unusual noise, overheating, vibration, strange smells, discoloration, incorrect pressure, etc.		
	IV	• Adhesion	Accumulation of debris, peeling, malfunction, etc.		
	V	• Contamination; Damage	Light powder, accumulation of dirt, rust, grease, oil; impact areas, dents, scratches, scuffs, etc.		
			Minor Flaws: Category Subtotal:	Score: divided by 5	
UNFULFILLED BASIC CONDITIONS	VI	• Lubrication	Insufficient lubrication, dirty oil, undetermined liquid, or leaking lubricant, etc.		
	VII	• Lubricant supply	Lubricant inlets; dirty, damaged, or deformed, faulty pipes, etc.		
	VIII	• Oil level guages	Dirty, leaking, or damaged, no measurement of correct level, etc.		
	IX	• Tightening	Fasteners; nuts, bolts; loose, missing, cross-threaded, crushed, corroded, etc.		
			Unfulfilled Basic Conditions: Category Subtotal:	Score: divided by 4	
INACCESSIBLE PLACES	X	• Cleaning	Machine, covers, space, layout of machine, space to be able to clean, etc.		
	XI	• Checking	Able to check, layout, instrument location, position and orientation, operating-range known, etc.		
	XII	• Lubricating	Location and position of lubricant nipples, height, lubricant outlet, enough space, etc.		
	XIII	• Operation	Machine layout; position of valves, switches and levers, etc.		
	XIV	• Adjustment	For adjustment, position of gauges, thermometers, flow-meters, moisture and vacuum gauges, etc.		
			Inaccessible Places: Category Subtotal:	Score: divided by 5	
CONTAMINATION SOURCES	XV	• Product, Raw material	Leaks from products, spilling and mixing product type; Scattered material, too much material, etc.		
	XVI	• Lubricants	Mixing with product, leaks causing contamination, seeping oils, fluids, etc.		
	XVII	• Gases	Lack of pressure, leaking air, gases, steam, vapors, exhaust fumes, etc.		
	XVIII	• Liquids	Leaking waste liquids, not cleaning with solvents, contaminates not out of fluids, etc.		
	XIX	• Scrap, Other	Dunnage, cuttings, non-conforming parts, contaminants by people, forklifts, etc.		
			Contamination Sources: Category Subtotal:	Score: divided by 5	
QUALITY DEFECT SOURCES	XX	• Moisture	Moisture source, too much, too little, infiltration, temperature change, humidity change, etc.		
	XXI	• Grain size	Right sized filters, old filters, defective filters, operation not considered, etc.		
	XXII	• Concentration, Viscosity	Inadequate acclimation, pre-heating, compounding; Mixing, evaporation, accumulation, stirring, etc.		
	XXIII	• Foreign matter, Shock	Inclusion, entrant of contaminants, chips, scraps; Dropping, jolting, collision, vibration, etc.		
			Quality Defect Sources: Category Subtotal:	Score: divided by 4	
UNNECESSARY AND NON-URGENT ITEMS	XXIV	• Machinery	Evaluate the hydraulic pumps, their fans, compressors, support columns, tanks, etc.		
	XXV	• Piping equipment	Address pipes, hoses, ducts, valves, dampers, etc.		
	XXVI	• Measuring instruments	Temperatures, pressure gauges, vacuum gauges, amp-meters, etc.		
	XXVII	• Electrical equipment	Wiring, piping, power leads, switches, plugs, etc.		
	XXVIII	• Jigs and tools	General tools, cutting tools, jigs, molds, dies, frames, etc.		
			Unnecessary and Non-urgent Items: Category Subtotal:	Score: divided by 5	
UNSAFE PLACES	XXIX	• Floors	Cracks, uneven floors, objects, peeling of material, etc.		
	XXX	• Steps	No slip, no handrails, irregular, uneven, too thin, slippery, etc.		
	XXXI	• Lights	Lack of lighting, no protection, dusty and grimy covers, missing lights, etc.		
	XXXII	• Rotating machinery	No protective covers, safety lines, safety cages, no emergency stops, etc.		
	XXXIII	• Lifting gear, Other	Location of hazards, wires, nail heads, split corners, other parts; Solvents, toxic gases, danger signs.		
			Unsafe Places: Category Subtotal:	Score: divided by 5	

Total "Category Subtotals" Divided by 33 Score: TOTAL

Abnormality Assessment Form

Date: _____   Evaluation Area: _____

Abnormality	Number	Evaluation Criteria	Rank these items from 1 through 5: 5 being well done	Score (1-5)	Ideas / Suggestions / Comments
MINOR FLAWS	I	• Damage	Cracking, crushing, deformation, chipping, bending, etc.		
	II	• Play, Slackness	Movement, falling out, tilting, eccentricity, distortion, corrosion; Drive belts, Drive chains, cables, etc.		
	III	• Abnormal phenomena	Unusual noise, overheating, vibration, strange smells, discoloration, incorrect pressure, etc.		
	IV	• Adhesion	Accumulation of debris, peeling, malfunction, etc.		
	V	• Contamination; Damage	Light powder, accumulation of dirt, rust, grease, oil; impact areas, dents, scratches, scuffs, etc.		
		Minor Flaws: Category Subtotal:	**Score: divided by 5**		
UNFULFILLED BASIC CONDITIONS	VI	• Lubrication	Insufficient lubrication, dirty oil, undetermined liquid, or leaking lubricant, etc.		
	VII	• Lubricant supply	Lubricant inlets; dirty, damaged, or deformed, faulty pipes, etc.		
	VIII	• Oil level guages	Dirty, leaking, or damaged, no measurement of correct level, etc.		
	IX	• Tightening	Fasteners; nuts, bolts; loose, missing, cross-threaded, crushed, corroded, etc.		
		Unfulfilled Basic Conditions: Category Subtotal:	**Score: divided by 4**		
INACCESSIBLE PLACES	X	• Cleaning	Machine, covers, space, layout of machine, space to be able to clean, etc.		
	XI	• Checking	Able to check, layout, instrument location, position and orientation, operating-range known, etc.		
	XII	• Lubricating	Location and position of lubricant nipples, height, lubricant outlet, enough space, etc.		
	XIII	• Operation	Machine layout; position of valves, switches and levers, etc.		
	XIV	• Adjustment	For adjustment, position of gauges, thermometers, flow-meters, moisture and vacuum gauges, etc.		
		Inaccessible Places: Category Subtotal:	**Score: divided by 5**		
CONTAMINATION SOURCES	XV	• Product, Raw material	Leaks from products, spilling and mixing product type; Scattered material, too much material, etc.		
	XVI	• Lubricants	Mixing with product, leaks causing contamination, seeping oils, fluids, etc.		
	XVII	• Gases	Lack of pressure, leaking air, gases, steam, vapors, exhaust fumes, etc.		
	XVIII	• Liquids	Leaking waste liquids, not cleaning with solvents, contaminates not out of fluids, etc.		
	XIX	• Scrap, Other	Dunnage, cuttings, non-conforming parts, contaminants by people, forklifts, etc.		
		Contamination Sources: Category Subtotal:	**Score: divided by 5**		
QUALITY DEFECT SOURCES	XX	• Moisture	Moisture source, too much, too little, infiltration, temperature change, humidity change, etc.		
	XXI	• Grain size	Right sized filters, old filters, defective filters, operation not considered, etc.		
	XXII	• Concentration, Viscosity	Inadequate acclimation, pre-heating, compounding; Mixing, evaporation, accumulation, stirring, etc.		
	XXIII	• Foreign matter, Shock	Inclusion, entrant of contaminants, chips, scraps; Dropping, jolting, collision, vibration, etc.		
		Quality Defect Sources: Category Subtotal:	**Score: divided by 4**		
UNNECESSARY AND NON-URGENT ITEMS	XXIV	• Machinery	Evaluate the hydraulic pumps, their fans, compressors, support columns, tanks, etc.		
	XXV	• Piping equipment	Address pipes, hoses, ducts, valves, dampers, etc.		
	XXVI	• Measuring instruments	Temperatures, pressure gauges, vacuum gauges, amp-meters, etc.		
	XXVII	• Electrical equipment	Wiring, piping, power leads, switches, plugs, etc.		
	XXVIII	• Jigs and tools	General tools, cutting tools, jigs, molds, dies, frames, etc.		
		Unnecessary and Non-urgent Items: Category Subtotal:	**Score: divided by 5**		
UNSAFE PLACES	XXIX	• Floors	Cracks, uneven floors, objects, peeling of material, etc.		
	XXX	• Steps	No slip, no handrails, irregular, uneven, too thin, slippery, etc.		
	XXXI	• Lights	Lack of lighting, no protection, dusty and grimy covers, missing lights, etc.		
	XXXII	• Rotating machinery	No protective covers, safety lines, safety cages, no emergency stops, etc.		
	XXXIII	• Lifting gear, Other	Location of hazards, wires, nail heads, split corners, other parts; Solvents, toxic gases, danger signs.		
		Unsafe Places: Category Subtotal:	**Score: divided by 5**		

Total "Category Subtotals" Divided by 33 Score: TOTAL

Abnormality Assessment Form

Date: _____   Evaluation Area: _____

Abnormality	Number	Evaluation Criteria	Rank these items from 1 through 5: 5 being well done	Score (1-5)	Ideas / Suggestions / Comments
MINOR FLAWS	I	• Damage	Cracking, crushing, deformation, chipping, bending, etc.		
	II	• Play, Slackness	Movement, falling out, tilting, eccentricity, distortion, corrosion; Drive belts, Drive chains, cables, etc.		
	III	• Abnormal phenomena	Unusual noise, overheating, vibration, strange smells, discoloration, incorrect pressure, etc.		
	IV	• Adhesion	Accumulation of debris, peeling, malfunction, etc.		
	V	• Contamination; Damage	Light powder, accumulation of dirt, rust, grease, oil; impact areas, dents, scratches, scuffs, etc.		
			Minor Flaws: Category Subtotal: Score: divided by 5		
UNFULFILLED BASIC CONDITIONS	VI	• Lubrication	Insufficient lubrication, dirty oil, undetermined liquid, or leaking lubricant, etc.		
	VII	• Lubricant supply	Lubricant inlets; dirty, damaged, or deformed, faulty pipes, etc.		
	VIII	• Oil level guages	Dirty, leaking, or damaged, no measurement of correct level, etc.		
	IX	• Tightening	Fasteners; nuts, bolts; loose, missing, cross-threaded, crushed, corroded, etc.		
			Unfulfilled Basic Conditions: Category Subtotal: Score: divided by 4		
INACCESSIBLE PLACES	X	• Cleaning	Machine, covers, space, layout of machine, space to be able to clean, etc.		
	XI	• Checking	Able to check, layout, instrument location, position and orientation, operating-range known, etc.		
	XII	• Lubricating	Location and position of lubricant nipples, height, lubricant outlet, enough space, etc.		
	XIII	• Operation	Machine layout; position of valves, switches and levers, etc.		
	XIV	• Adjustment	For adjustment, position of gauges, thermometers, flow-meters, moisture and vacuum gauges, etc.		
			Inaccessible Places: Category Subtotal: Score: divided by 5		
CONTAMINATION SOURCES	XV	• Product, Raw material	Leaks from products, spilling and mixing product type; Scattered material, too much material, etc.		
	XVI	• Lubricants	Mixing with product, leaks causing contamination, seeping oils, fluids, etc.		
	XVII	• Gases	Lack of pressure, leaking air, gases, steam, vapors, exhaust fumes, etc.		
	XVIII	• Liquids	Leaking waste liquids, not cleaning with solvents, contaminates not out of fluids, etc.		
	XIX	• Scrap, Other	Dunnage, cuttings, non-conforming parts, contaminants by people, forklifts, etc.		
			Contamination Sources: Category Subtotal: Score: divided by 5		
QUALITY DEFECT SOURCES	XX	• Moisture	Moisture source, too much, too little, infiltration, temperature change, humidity change, etc.		
	XXI	• Grain size	Right sized filters, old filters, defective filters, operation not considered, etc.		
	XXII	• Concentration, Viscosity	Inadequate acclimation, pre-heating, compounding; Mixing, evaporation, accumulation, stirring, etc.		
	XXIII	• Foreign matter, Shock	Inclusion, entrant of contaminants, chips, scraps; Dropping, jolting, collision, vibration, etc.		
			Quality Defect Sources: Category Subtotal: Score: divided by 4		
UNNECESSARY AND NON-URGENT ITEMS	XXIV	• Machinery	Evaluate the hydraulic pumps, their fans, compressors, support columns, tanks, etc.		
	XXV	• Piping equipment	Address pipes, hoses, ducts, valves, dampers, etc.		
	XXVI	• Measuring instruments	Temperatures, pressure gauges, vacuum gauges, amp-meters, etc.		
	XXVII	• Electrical equipment	Wiring, piping, power leads, switches, plugs, etc.		
	XXVIII	• Jigs and tools	General tools, cutting tools, jigs, molds, dies, frames, etc.		
			Unnecessary and Non-urgent Items: Category Subtotal: Score: divided by 5		
UNSAFE PLACES	XXIX	• Floors	Cracks, uneven floors, objects, peeling of material, etc.		
	XXX	• Steps	No slip, no handrails, irregular, uneven, too thin, slippery, etc.		
	XXXI	• Lights	Lack of lighting, no protection, dusty and grimy covers, missing lights, etc.		
	XXXII	• Rotating machinery	No protective covers, safety lines, safety cages, no emergency stops, etc.		
	XXXIII	• Lifting gear, Other	Location of hazards, wires, nail heads, split corners, other parts; Solvents, toxic gases, danger signs.		
			Unsafe Places: Category Subtotal: Score: divided by 5		

© ENNA
KNOWLEDGE INTO PRACTICE
www.enna.com
www.productivitypress.com

Total "Category Subtotals" Divided by 33 Score: TOTAL

Abnormality Assessment Form

Date: _____ Evaluation Area: _____

Abnormality	Number	Evaluation Criteria	Rank these items from 1 through 5: 5 being well done	Score (1-5)	Ideas / Suggestions / Comments
MINOR FLAWS	I	• Damage	Cracking, crushing, deformation, chipping, bending, etc.		
	II	• Play, Slackness	Movement, falling out, tilting, eccentricity, distortion, corrosion; Drive belts, Drive chains, cables, etc.		
	III	• Abnormal phenomena	Unusual noise, overheating, vibration, strange smells, discoloration, incorrect pressure, etc.		
	IV	• Adhesion	Accumulation of debris, peeling, malfunction, etc.		
	V	• Contamination; Damage	Light powder, accumulation of dirt, rust, grease, oil; impact areas, dents, scratches, scuffs, etc.		
			Minor Flaws: Category Subtotal: Score: divided by 5		
UNFULFILLED BASIC CONDITIONS	VI	• Lubrication	Insufficient lubrication, dirty oil, undetermined liquid, or leaking lubricant, etc.		
	VII	• Lubricant supply	Lubricant inlets; dirty, damaged, or deformed, faulty pipes, etc.		
	VIII	• Oil level guages	Dirty, leaking, or damaged, no measurement of correct level, etc.		
	IX	• Tightening	Fasteners; nuts, bolts; loose, missing, cross-threaded, crushed, corroded, etc.		
			Unfulfilled Basic Conditions: Category Subtotal: Score: divided by 4		
INACCESSIBLE PLACES	X	• Cleaning	Machine, covers, space, layout of machine, space to be able to clean, etc.		
	XI	• Checking	Able to check, layout, instrument location, position and orientation, operating-range known, etc.		
	XII	• Lubricating	Location and position of lubricant nipples, height, lubricant outlet, enough space, etc.		
	XIII	• Operation	Machine layout; position of valves, switches and levers, etc.		
	XIV	• Adjustment	For adjustment, position of gauges, thermometers, flow-meters, moisture and vacuum gauges, etc.		
			Inaccessible Places: Category Subtotal: Score: divided by 5		
CONTAMINATION SOURCES	XV	• Product, Raw material	Leaks from products, spilling and mixing product type; Scattered material, too much material, etc.		
	XVI	• Lubricants	Mixing with product, leaks causing contamination, seeping oils, fluids, etc.		
	XVII	• Gases	Lack of pressure, leaking air, gases, steam, vapors, exhaust fumes, etc.		
	XVIII	• Liquids	Leaking waste liquids, not cleaning with solvents, contaminates not out of fluids, etc.		
	XIX	• Scrap, Other	Dunnage, cuttings, non-conforming parts, contaminants by people, forklifts, etc.		
			Contamination Sources: Category Subtotal: Score: divided by 5		
QUALITY DEFECT SOURCES	XX	• Moisture	Moisture source, too much, too little, infiltration, temperature change, humidity change, etc.		
	XXI	• Grain size	Right sized filters, old filters, defective filters, operation not considered, etc.		
	XXII	• Concentration, Viscosity	Inadequate acclimation, pre-heating, compounding; Mixing, evaporation, accumulation, stirring, etc.		
	XXIII	• Foreign matter, Shock	Inclusion, entrant of contaminants, chips, scraps; Dropping, jolting, collision, vibration, etc.		
			Quality Defect Sources: Category Subtotal: Score: divided by 4		
UNNECESSARY AND NON-URGENT ITEMS	XXIV	• Machinery	Evaluate the hydraulic pumps, their fans, compressors, support columns, tanks, etc.		
	XXV	• Piping equipment	Address pipes, hoses, ducts, valves, dampers, etc.		
	XXVI	• Measuring instruments	Temperatures, pressure gauges, vacuum gauges, amp-meters, etc.		
	XXVII	• Electrical equipment	Wiring, piping, power leads, switches, plugs, etc.		
	XXVIII	• Jigs and tools	General tools, cutting tools, jigs, molds, dies, frames, etc.		
			Unnecessary and Non-urgent Items: Category Subtotal: Score: divided by 5		
UNSAFE PLACES	XXIX	• Floors	Cracks, uneven floors, objects, peeling of material, etc.		
	XXX	• Steps	No slip, no handrails, irregular, uneven, too thin, slippery, etc.		
	XXXI	• Lights	Lack of lighting, no protection, dusty and grimy covers, missing lights, etc.		
	XXXII	• Rotating machinery	No protective covers, safety lines, safety cages, no emergency stops, etc.		
	XXXIII	• Lifting gear, Other	Location of hazards, wires, nail heads, split corners, other parts; Solvents, toxic gases, danger signs.		
			Unsafe Places: Category Subtotal: Score: divided by 5		

Total "Category Subtotals" Divided by 33 Score: TOTAL

Abnormality Assessment Form

Date: _____ Evaluation Area: _____

Abnormality	Number	Evaluation Criteria	Rank these items from 1 through 5: 5 being well done	Score (1-5)	Ideas / Suggestions / Comments
MINOR FLAWS	I	• Damage	Cracking, crushing, deformation, chipping, bending, etc.		
	II	• Play, Slackness	Movement, falling out, tilting, eccentricity, distortion, corrosion; Drive belts, Drive chains, cables, etc.		
	III	• Abnormal phenomena	Unusual noise, overheating, vibration, strange smells, discoloration, incorrect pressure, etc.		
	IV	• Adhesion	Accumulation of debris, peeling, malfunction, etc.		
	V	• Contamination; Damage	Light powder, accumulation of dirt, rust, grease, oil; impact areas, dents, scratches, scuffs, etc.		
			Minor Flaws: Category Subtotal:	Score: divided by 5	
UNFULFILLED BASIC CONDITIONS	VI	• Lubrication	Insufficient lubrication, dirty oil, undetermined liquid, or leaking lubricant, etc.		
	VII	• Lubricant supply	Lubricant inlets; dirty, damaged, or deformed, faulty pipes, etc.		
	VIII	• Oil level guages	Dirty, leaking, or damaged, no measurement of correct level, etc.		
	IX	• Tightening	Fasteners; nuts, bolts; loose, missing, cross-threaded, crushed, corroded, etc.		
			Unfulfilled Basic Conditions: Category Subtotal:	Score: divided by 4	
INACCESSIBLE PLACES	X	• Cleaning	Machine, covers, space, layout of machine, space to be able to clean, etc.		
	XI	• Checking	Able to check, layout, instrument location, position and orientation, operating-range known, etc.		
	XII	• Lubricating	Location and position of lubricant nipples, height, lubricant outlet, enough space, etc.		
	XIII	• Operation	Machine layout; position of valves, switches and levers, etc.		
	XIV	• Adjustment	For adjustment, position of gauges, thermometers, flow-meters, moisture and vacuum gauges, etc.		
			Inaccessible Places: Category Subtotal:	Score: divided by 5	
CONTAMINATION SOURCES	XV	• Product, Raw material	Leaks from products, spilling and mixing product type; Scattered material, too much material, etc.		
	XVI	• Lubricants	Mixing with product, leaks causing contamination, seeping oils, fluids, etc.		
	XVII	• Gases	Lack of pressure, leaking air, gases, steam, vapors, exhaust fumes, etc.		
	XVIII	• Liquids	Leaking waste liquids, not cleaning with solvents, contaminates not out of fluids, etc.		
	XIX	• Scrap, Other	Dunnage, cuttings, non-conforming parts, contaminants by people, forklifts, etc.		
			Contamination Sources: Category Subtotal:	Score: divided by 5	
QUALITY DEFECT SOURCES	XX	• Moisture	Moisture source, too much, too little, infiltration, temperature change, humidity change, etc.		
	XXI	• Grain size	Right sized filters, old filters, defective filters, operation not considered, etc.		
	XXII	• Concentration, Viscosity	Inadequate acclimation, pre-heating, compounding; Mixing, evaporation, accumulation, stirring, etc.		
	XXIII	• Foreign matter, Shock	Inclusion, entrant of contaminants, chips, scraps; Dropping, jolting, collision, vibration, etc.		
			Quality Defect Sources: Category Subtotal:	Score: divided by 4	
UNNECESSARY AND NON-URGENT ITEMS	XXIV	• Machinery	Evaluate the hydraulic pumps, their fans, compressors, support columns, tanks, etc.		
	XXV	• Piping equipment	Address pipes, hoses, ducts, valves, dampers, etc.		
	XXVI	• Measuring instruments	Temperatures, pressure gauges, vacuum gauges, amp-meters, etc.		
	XXVII	• Electrical equipment	Wiring, piping, power leads, switches, plugs, etc.		
	XXVIII	• Jigs and tools	General tools, cutting tools, jigs, molds, dies, frames, etc.		
			Unnecessary and Non-urgent Items: Category Subtotal:	Score: divided by 5	
UNSAFE PLACES	XXIX	• Floors	Cracks, uneven floors, objects, peeling of material, etc.		
	XXX	• Steps	No slip, no handrails, irregular, uneven, too thin, slippery, etc.		
	XXXI	• Lights	Lack of lighting, no protection, dusty and grimy covers, missing lights, etc.		
	XXXII	• Rotating machinery	No protective covers, safety lines, safety cages, no emergency stops, etc.		
	XXXIII	• Lifting gear, Other	Location of hazards, wires, nail heads, split corners, other parts; Solvents, toxic gases, danger signs.		
			Unsafe Places: Category Subtotal:	Score: divided by 5	

Total "Category Subtotals" Divided by 33 Score: TOTAL

Abnormality Assessment Form

Date: _____   Evaluation Area: _____

Abnormality	Number	Evaluation Criteria	Rank these items from 1 through 5: 5 being well done	Score (1-5)	Ideas / Suggestions / Comments
MINOR FLAWS	I	• Damage	Cracking, crushing, deformation, chipping, bending, etc.		
	II	• Play, Slackness	Movement, falling out, tilting, eccentricity, distortion, corrosion; Drive belts, Drive chains, cables, etc.		
	III	• Abnormal phenomena	Unusual noise, overheating, vibration, strange smells, discoloration, incorrect pressure, etc.		
	IV	• Adhesion	Accumulation of debris, peeling, malfunction, etc.		
	V	• Contamination; Damage	Light powder, accumulation of dirt, rust, grease, oil; impact areas, dents, scratches, scuffs, etc.		
			Minor Flaws: Category Subtotal:	Score: divided by 5	
UNFULFILLED BASIC CONDITIONS	VI	• Lubrication	Insufficient lubrication, dirty oil, undetermined liquid, or leaking lubricant, etc.		
	VII	• Lubricant supply	Lubricant inlets; dirty, damaged, or deformed, faulty pipes, etc.		
	VIII	• Oil level guages	Dirty, leaking, or damaged, no measurement of correct level, etc.		
	IX	• Tightening	Fasteners; nuts, bolts; loose, missing, cross-threaded, crushed, corroded, etc.		
			Unfulfilled Basic Conditions: Category Subtotal:	Score: divided by 4	
INACCESSIBLE PLACES	X	• Cleaning	Machine, covers, space, layout of machine, space to be able to clean, etc.		
	XI	• Checking	Able to check, layout, instrument location, position and orientation, operating-range known, etc.		
	XII	• Lubricating	Location and position of lubricant nipples, height, lubricant outlet, enough space, etc.		
	XIII	• Operation	Machine layout; position of valves, switches and levers, etc.		
	XIV	• Adjustment	For adjustment, position of gauges, thermometers, flow-meters, moisture and vacuum gauges, etc.		
			Inaccessible Places: Category Subtotal:	Score: divided by 5	
CONTAMINATION SOURCES	XV	• Product, Raw material	Leaks from products, spilling and mixing product type; Scattered material, too much material, etc.		
	XVI	• Lubricants	Mixing with product, leaks causing contamination, seeping oils, fluids, etc.		
	XVII	• Gases	Lack of pressure, leaking air, gases, steam, vapors, exhaust fumes, etc.		
	XVIII	• Liquids	Leaking waste liquids, not cleaning with solvents, contaminates not out of fluids, etc.		
	XIX	• Scrap, Other	Dunnage, cuttings, non-conforming parts, contaminants by people, forklifts, etc.		
			Contamination Sources: Category Subtotal:	Score: divided by 5	
QUALITY DEFECT SOURCES	XX	• Moisture	Moisture source, too much, too little, infiltration, temperature change, humidity change, etc.		
	XXI	• Grain size	Right sized filters, old filters, defective filters, operation not considered, etc.		
	XXII	• Concentration, Viscosity	Inadequate acclimation, pre-heating, compounding; Mixing, evaporation, accumulation, stirring, etc.		
	XXIII	• Foreign matter, Shock	Inclusion, entrant of contaminants, chips, scraps; Dropping, jolting, collision, vibration, etc.		
			Quality Defect Sources: Category Subtotal:	Score: divided by 4	
UNNECESSARY AND NON-URGENT ITEMS	XXIV	• Machinery	Evaluate the hydraulic pumps, their fans, compressors, support columns, tanks, etc.		
	XXV	• Piping equipment	Address pipes, hoses, ducts, valves, dampers, etc.		
	XXVI	• Measuring instruments	Temperatures, pressure gauges, vacuum gauges, amp-meters, etc.		
	XXVII	• Electrical equipment	Wiring, piping, power leads, switches, plugs, etc.		
	XXVIII	• Jigs and tools	General tools, cutting tools, jigs, molds, dies, frames, etc.		
			Unnecessary and Non-urgent Items: Category Subtotal:	Score: divided by 5	
UNSAFE PLACES	XXIX	• Floors	Cracks, uneven floors, objects, peeling of material, etc.		
	XXX	• Steps	No slip, no handrails, irregular, uneven, too thin, slippery, etc.		
	XXXI	• Lights	Lack of lighting, no protection, dusty and grimy covers, missing lights, etc.		
	XXXII	• Rotating machinery	No protective covers, safety lines, safety cages, no emergency stops, etc.		
	XXXIII	• Lifting gear, Other	Location of hazards, wires, nail heads, split corners, other parts; Solvents, toxic gases, danger signs.		
			Unsafe Places: Category Subtotal:	Score: divided by 5	

Total "Category Subtotals" Divided by 33 Score: TOTAL

Abnormality Assessment Form

Date: _____ Evaluation Area: _____

Abnormality	Number	Evaluation Criteria	Rank these items from 1 through 5: 5 being well done	Score (1-5)	Ideas / Suggestions / Comments
MINOR FLAWS	I	• Damage	Cracking, crushing, deformation, chipping, bending, etc.		
	II	• Play, Slackness	Movement, falling out, tilting, eccentricity, distortion, corrosion; Drive belts, Drive chains, cables, etc.		
	III	• Abnormal phenomena	Unusual noise, overheating, vibration, strange smells, discoloration, incorrect pressure, etc.		
	IV	• Adhesion	Accumulation of debris, peeling, malfunction, etc.		
	V	• Contamination; Damage	Light powder, accumulation of dirt, rust, grease, oil; impact areas, dents, scratches, scuffs, etc.		
			Minor Flaws: Category Subtotal: Score: divided by 5		
UNFULFILLED BASIC CONDITIONS	VI	• Lubrication	Insufficient lubrication, dirty oil, undetermined liquid, or leaking lubricant, etc.		
	VII	• Lubricant supply	Lubricant inlets; dirty, damaged, or deformed, faulty pipes, etc.		
	VIII	• Oil level guages	Dirty, leaking, or damaged, no measurement of correct level, etc.		
	IX	• Tightening	Fasteners; nuts, bolts; loose, missing, cross-threaded, crushed, corroded, etc.		
			Unfulfilled Basic Conditions: Category Subtotal: Score: divided by 4		
INACCESSIBLE PLACES	X	• Cleaning	Machine, covers, space, layout of machine, space to be able to clean, etc.		
	XI	• Checking	Able to check, layout, instrument location, position and orientation, operating-range known, etc.		
	XII	• Lubricating	Location and position of lubricant nipples, height, lubricant outlet, enough space, etc.		
	XIII	• Operation	Machine layout; position of valves, switches and levers, etc.		
	XIV	• Adjustment	For adjustment, position of gauges, thermometers, flow-meters, moisture and vacuum gauges, etc.		
			Inaccessible Places: Category Subtotal: Score: divided by 5		
CONTAMINATION SOURCES	XV	• Product, Raw material	Leaks from products, spilling and mixing product type; Scattered material, too much material, etc.		
	XVI	• Lubricants	Mixing with product, leaks causing contamination, seeping oils, fluids, etc.		
	XVII	• Gases	Lack of pressure, leaking air, gases, steam, vapors, exhaust fumes, etc.		
	XVIII	• Liquids	Leaking waste liquids, not cleaning with solvents, contaminates not out of fluids, etc.		
	XIX	• Scrap, Other	Dunnage, cuttings, non-conforming parts, contaminants by people, forklifts, etc.		
			Contamination Sources: Category Subtotal: Score: divided by 5		
QUALITY DEFECT SOURCES	XX	• Moisture	Moisture source, too much, too little, infiltration, temperature change, humidity change, etc.		
	XXI	• Grain size	Right sized filters, old filters, defective filters, operation not considered, etc.		
	XXII	• Concentration, Viscosity	Inadequate acclimation, pre-heating, compounding; Mixing, evaporation, accumulation, stirring, etc.		
	XXIII	• Foreign matter, Shock	Inclusion, entrant of contaminants, chips, scraps; Dropping, jolting, collision, vibration, etc.		
			Quality Defect Sources: Category Subtotal: Score: divided by 4		
UNNECESSARY AND NON-URGENT ITEMS	XXIV	• Machinery	Evaluate the hydraulic pumps, their fans, compressors, support columns, tanks, etc.		
	XXV	• Piping equipment	Address pipes, hoses, ducts, valves, dampers, etc.		
	XXVI	• Measuring instruments	Temperatures, pressure gauges, vacuum gauges, amp-meters, etc.		
	XXVII	• Electrical equipment	Wiring, piping, power leads, switches, plugs, etc.		
	XXVIII	• Jigs and tools	General tools, cutting tools, jigs, molds, dies, frames, etc.		
			Unnecessary and Non-urgent Items: Category Subtotal: Score: divided by 5		
UNSAFE PLACES	XXIX	• Floors	Cracks, uneven floors, objects, peeling of material, etc.		
	XXX	• Steps	No slip, no handrails, irregular, uneven, too thin, slippery, etc.		
	XXXI	• Lights	Lack of lighting, no protection, dusty and grimy covers, missing lights, etc.		
	XXXII	• Rotating machinery	No protective covers, safety lines, safety cages, no emergency stops, etc.		
	XXXIII	• Lifting gear, Other	Location of hazards, wires, nail heads, split corners, other parts; Solvents, toxic gases, danger signs.		
			Unsafe Places: Category Subtotal: Score: divided by 5		

Total "Category Subtotals" Divided by 33 Score: TOTAL

www.enna.com
www.productivitypress.com